W9-CCV-371

# Howard Strong

## What Every
# Credit
# Card
## User Needs
## to Know

*How to Protect Yourself and Your Money*

AN OWL BOOK

HENRY HOLT AND COMPANY • NEW YORK

HG
3755
.S746
1999

Henry Holt and Company, Inc.
*Publishers since 1866*
115 West 18th Street
New York, New York 10011

Henry Holt® is a registered trademark
of Henry Holt and Company, Inc.

Published in Canada by Fitzhenry & Whiteside Ltd.,
195 Allstate Parkway, Markham, Ontario L3R 4T8.

---

WARNING: The law is *very* complex. Your situation
may differ from those in this book, or the law
may have changed. For advice on your personal
legal situation consult a local attorney.

---

Library of Congress Cataloging-in-Publication Data
Strong, Howard.
    What every credit card user needs to know : how to protect
yourself and your money / Howard Strong.
        p.      cm.
    Includes bibliographical references and index.
    ISBN 0-8050-5314-X (pbk. : alk. paper)
    1. Credit cards. 2. Consumer credit. 3. Finance, Personal.
I. Title.
HG3755.S746    1998
332.7'65—dc21                                    98-24343

Henry Holt books are available for special promotions
and premiums. For details contact: Director, Special Markets.

First Edition 1999

Designed by Victoria Hartman

Printed in the United States of America
All first editions are printed on acid-free paper.∞

10  9  8  7  6  5  4  3  2  1

This book is dedicated to my mother,
Betty Lou Strange (1926–1998).

"God could not be everywhere
so he created mothers."
—attributed to *Maimonides*

# Contents

# Introduction

Congratulations. In buying this book you have put yourself in position to take control of a most important part of your life: your personal finances. Many credit card users have neither the desire nor the knowledge to get the best possible money-saving deals around. Or to avoid the costly and dangerous rip-offs that are hiding everywhere in the credit card jungle. And they pay out big bucks for nothing because of this failure.

You, in contrast, by getting this book have shown that you do have the desire to get what you should for your hard-earned money. This book will give you the knowledge you must have to take charge of your credit card life.

Credit card users are being abused—by the credit card companies, by the merchants, by the government. I wrote this book to help stop that abuse. You can fight back and win! But first you have to know *how* you are being abused.

My files are full of newspaper and magazine stories about the rights of credit card users. Unfortunately, those stories often don't tell you what your rights really are and what really goes on. One, they give you incomplete (and often just plain wrong) information about your credit card legal rights. Two, they assume that the card companies usually obey the law.

But many credit card companies *don't* obey the law. They ignore it because they think they can get away with it and make bigger profits doing so. Demanding your legal rights from some corporation that has no intention of letting you have them is useless unless you know how to push that corporation to obey the law.

This book tells you what your credit card rights really are and the best way to get them. Read on and learn how to handle the credit card companies.

There are laws that protect you when you get and when you use your credit card. Some of these laws are not strong enough, but even so, they can be very useful to you if you know what they are and how to use them.

This book tells you about the applicable laws and explains how you can make the easiest and most effective use of them to protect yourself against credit card companies and merchants who do not deliver what you pay for. It also tells you how to choose the best card for yourself and gives you lots of tips for profiting from your cards and for avoiding the financial disaster that is, for the unknowing, hiding in those bright-colored plastic rectangles.

*What Every Credit Card User Needs to Know* is exclusively about credit cards. There is nothing about other kinds of consumer credit in here. No home loans, car financing, or furniture payments—unless these are tied into credit cards.

This book is not about how to take wrongful advantage of the system. Anyone looking for a something-for-nothing plan or a guide to how to pull off scams on a credit card company should stop reading here. You who want to know about your legal rights, read on. To learn how you are being ripped off and who is doing the ripping. Find out how you can strike back at the rip-off artists.

### How I Got Into Credit Cards

Like most folks, I started out knowing nothing about credit cards. Many years ago I was living in Paris and doing my banking with a big American bank with an office there in France. I used their credit card for lots of things. Some problems developed—incorrect bills, for one. The bank didn't seem to have much interest in working things out. I was a lawyer, but I (like most lawyers) knew little about credit card law. So I looked for a book to explain it to me and help me solve the billing problems. I discovered there was no layperson's guide to credit card rights. So after doing some research and resolving the billing problems I decided to write one. *Et voilà!*

Doing the research for that first book (eventually published in 1989 as *Credit Card Secrets*) was extremely educational. When I returned to the States, I got involved in defending consumers against credit card companies and have now worked on many such cases, including several important class-action suits.

## Why I Love Credit Cards

As you read this book, with its parade of horribles, you might get the impression that I am against credit cards. Not so. Credit cards are great if you know how to use them to your benefit and how to exercise your legal rights if you need to.

Credit cards can help simplify your financial life. Properly used, they can help you keep good records for budgeting and tax purposes. They can cut down on the amount of time you spend recording and managing money details. As a well-known animator told me at a Hollywood gathering: "I charge everything that can possibly be charged on my frequent-flier-mileage Visa card. Then at the end of each month I can put the charges into my Quicken program and see if I'm on budget. At the end of the year I can give the information to my tax guy and he has an accurate record of where my money went, which means extra deductions for me."

> As far as I was concerned, credit was the ultimate luxury. It wasn't what Thoreau had in mind, but more than anything else I'd ever experienced, it made life simple.
>
> —Lia Matera, *Prior Convictions*

Using credit cards also lets you pretty much avoid going to the bank or the automatic teller machine (ATM) to get cash. Your card is like a never-empty wallet you never have to go to the bank to refill (so long as you keep up with the bills). Use a credit card to pay for almost everything almost everywhere and you will have better records and stay out of lots of those nasty bank lines. Plus, you will have a lot of powerful consumer rights that you sure don't have if you pay cash. You may also find that it is easier to return purchases when the store can credit the return to your account (none of that waiting fourteen days for the check you used to pay for the returned item to clear before you get your refund). You will be in less danger of losing money to a mugger because you won't have much cash for the mugger to steal. You will be able to make big purchases without worrying about whether you have enough money in your checking account to cover the check. You can get a frequent-flier card and build up credit toward free airline tickets for travel to Pittsburgh or Paris. You (with the right card) can get free extended warranty protection on many of your purchases and free damage insurance on car rentals. And you can do things that are almost impossible to do without a credit card, such as check into a decent hotel or rent a car.

> Under the facade of the democratization of credit, lenders are expanding their business to borrowers with poor credit histories and to low-income, inner-city residents, who are often members of minority groups. Then, when the same borrowers default on their loans, these same lenders are the first to call them deadbeats and to cry to Congress that bankruptcy laws should be changed to force them to pay their debts.
> —Professor Fred Waddel of Auburn University
> writing in *The New York Times*

Yep, I love credit cards. Properly handled, they can ease your way though life. Improperly handled, they can ruin your financial life, as many of the students who come to my adult education class on resolving credit problems can certainly testify.

## The History of Credit Cards

Credit cards got going in the United States just before the start of World War I. Department stores started to issue dog-tag style metal plates to favorite customers. By 1924 you could fill up your Model T Ford using one of the new gas credit cards, the first that could be used at merchants around the country. This was an important advance, made necessary because a gas card that wasn't accepted when traveling was not very useful, and as cars became more common, so did traveling. Indeed, increasing American mobility is one of the reasons credit cards have become so popular. A merchant in Florida might refuse your Illinois check, but would take your American Express Card with no problems.

But the Depression made people cut way back on travel and buying, as did World War II, which brought rationing of tires and gas as well as government controls on credit.

Then came 1950 and the Diners Club. Francis X. McNamara, operator of a small loan company in New York City, ran across a fellow who had lots of department-store charge cards. He would lend them out to friends and charge for their use. He would borrow money from McNamara's loan operation and use it to pay off the card bills run up by his pals. He profited from the spread between the rate he paid McNamara and the interest rate his friends paid him.

Next, one of the friends failed to pay up and his enterprise collapsed, sticking McNamara with uncollectable debts. The story goes that McNamara was sitting around at lunch with his attorney talking about how to recover his losses when he was struck with the idea that led to the Diners Club. Why not a card that could be used at many merchants? Since the idea hit him in a restaurant, he decided to start with restaurants.

He issued a card—really a card: it was made from cardboard—with the holder's name and account number on the front and a list of the twenty-eight restaurants and Manhattan nightspots that accepted it on the back. The annual fee was five dollars.

McNamara got his lawyer, Ralph Schneider, to help him out with the business and Schneider hired a publicity agent, Marty Simmons, to drum up more restaurants and cardholders for Diners. Diners grew into the first national credit card not limited to just gas and oil.

In 1951 Franklin National Bank of New York created a credit card that could be used at all kinds of merchants (Diners was then restricted to restaurants, hotels, and air travel expenses). Other banks started their own programs, and then the giant Bank of America in San Francisco started its own BankAmericard, which later evolved into Visa. Other California banks started their own plans, which much later became MasterCard.

In 1958, American Express looked at Diners Club's profits and started its own card.

Next, BankAmericard really got rolling. Other banks saw there was big money in credit cards. Each wanted to have its own. But to have a credit card operation they had to have lots of customers. So at the end of the sixties the banks started mailing out cards to anyone with a name and an address. Dead or alive, creditworthy or not—this didn't matter to the bankers. Lots of people were getting and using the cards, some of them even the people whose names were on the cards. Credit card use rose and credit card fraud was rampant. Mail theft became a plague as crooks discovered that those envelopes with cards in them were just like envelopes full of cash. And there was little to stop card companies from sending out cards consumers had never asked for, cards consumers did not expect and could not know had been stolen until the card company demanded payment from John Doe for fraudulent charges on a card the bank had issued in Doe's name, although he had never asked for and never received or used the card.

I treasure the story about the consumer who got a call asking if she wanted to get a credit card from a major bank. She said, "Maybe later," and quickly received a card for Mabel Later.

Crime and other problems caused by this card pushing by the banks led directly to passage of the Fair Credit Billing Act of 1974 and many other consumer protection laws, laws still around to protect you.

### Card Law—What It Is

Until the seventies there wasn't much in the way of special credit card law because there weren't many credit cards around. Then abuse of card users by the card companies pushed Congress and the states to pass new consumer protection legislation. The federal laws, passed by Congress, cover the entire United States. The state laws, passed by various state legislatures, cover only things that happen in each individual state. So if you live in California and have a problem with a California-based credit card company, both the federal and California laws would apply. Many state laws also apply to out-of-state card companies dealing with local residents. Sometimes the state laws are stronger than the federal law; sometimes they are not. It all depends on the state.

It's not possible to cover the laws of fifty states, so this book concentrates on federal law. If you want to check out the laws of your individual state, your best bet is to go to your local county law library (most counties have one in the main county courthouse) or a local law-school library. Generally, start your research at the law library under "credit cards" or "consumer credit." Some states, such as California, have posted their laws on the Internet.

Federal credit card laws on consumer protection have three levels:

- First are the laws actually passed by Congress. These are mostly found in Title 15 of the United States Code starting at section 1601 (15 U.S.C. 1601 in lawyer's abbreviation) and include the Truth in Lending Act (the main credit card law) the Fair Debt Collection Practices Act, the Equal Credit Opportunity Act, the Fair Credit Reporting Act, and so on. Sometimes they are called, all together, the Consumer Credit Protection Act.
- Second, Federal Reserve Board regulations that interpret the Truth in Lending and other laws about consumer credit. There are hundreds of pages of these Fed rules in what's called Regulation Z. The Fed also has an *Official Staff Commentary on Regulation Z.* (You can get free copies of Regulation Z and the Staff Commentary; see p. 154 for the address.)
- Then on top of all these, there are hundreds of court decisions (found at your local law library) interpreting the Truth in Lending Act, Regulation Z, and the Staff Commentary.

The idea of this book is to distill all this law down into information you can use without spending the rest of your life in the law library. In some ways this book is like a help manual to a home computer. You want to know how to use the computer, not how the electrons do their little dances to make the whole thing work. This book provides practical information about credit cards that you can use right now, without worrying about how the legal system operates.* But remember, sometimes you *do* need a lawyer. *What Every Credit Card User Needs to Know* interprets the law in a practical way so that you will be not only

---

*If you want to look at the nuts and bolts of the law, the first place to look might be the National Consumer Law Center's *Law of Truth in Lending* book mentioned in the Resources section. It reprints the TILA, Regulation Z, and the Staff Commentary and exhaustively discusses, in very lawyerly language many of the case decisions. Or you can find the raw material of TILA and Fed Regulation Z in any good law library and some larger public libraries.

an educated card user, but a card user who is in a position to protect yourself against strong-arm tactics by credit card companies.

The examples and sample letters were written especially for this book as models for your own correspondence. In some cases they have been adapted from actual correspondence; in other cases they have been created based on my experience in litigating many credit card cases and in talking to many folks in the card business. In all cases, the names and other identifying information have been changed to protect both the innocent and the guilty.

So read on, inform yourself about the little known ins and outs of the credit card business, become a more knowledgeable card user, pay less of your money to credit card companies, and keep more in your pocket.

What Every
# Credit
# Card
User Needs
to **Know**

# Credit Card Basics:
# Choosing the Right Card for You

There are several kinds of credit cards in common use today: store cards (examples: Macy's, Marshall Fields, Gulf Oil); hybrid store/bank cards (Bloomingdale's Visa); bank cards (First Chicago Visa, Wells Fargo MasterCard); travel and entertainment cards (American Express, Diners); some crossbreeds (Discover Card). Each has its pros and cons. In this chapter, we'll first explore the general pros and cons of credit cards. Then, we'll get into specifics about the pluses and minuses of each.

## The Pros and Cons of Credit Cards

While there may be plenty of problems with credit cards they are often very useful and can certainly help you in your financial life.

*Credit Card Freebies.* One big advantage of using credit cards is that many cards today offer free stuff to encourage you to get or use one particular card. The card companies, as discussed in Chapter 3, prefer not to compete on interest rates and other card costs. So they have come up with stuff to hand out that is less expensive to them than cutting interest rates and fees would be. Some of that stuff can be very valuable to you *if* you pay your balance in full every month. If you don't pay your balance every month, the heavy interest you will pay to the card company is almost certain to far outweigh the value of the freebies you get.

The freebies take many forms:

• *Cash rebates* on purchases—say, 1 percent on annual purchases totaling over a certain amount and a smaller rebate on a smaller annual total. At the end of the year you get a credit or a check for the rebate amount.

• *Future purchase discounts* (usually only on store cards or store/bank hybrid cards). For example, Bloomingdale's provides bonus points that can add up to gift certificates for each charge. Eddie Bauer sends out certificates good for ten or more dollars off your next purchase when you use its card for a couple of hundred dollars' worth of charges. These programs can save you lots when you make substantial purchases at one retailer.

• *Frequent-flier bonus mileage—a 2 percent discount on everything you buy.* All the major airlines have credit cards affiliated with their frequent-flier programs. These are bank cards, not cards issued by the airline. The easiest way to join these programs is to pick up an application at the airport or airline city ticket office. Once you get one of these airline-affiliated cards, you will receive a frequent-flier mile for each dollar you charge. Those miles are worth about two cents each. Since you can use your frequent-flier Visa or MasterCard (American Express and Diners have similar programs with the advantage that their miles do not expire in three or so years as do miles on most of the other frequent-flier cards) to buy just about anything today, you can get miles on everything you spend. For example, I talked to a Chicago businessman who was building his family a new house. He charged more than $200,000 worth of materials on his airline card and got several free trips to Hawaii. He was careful to use a card with no mileage cap. Some of the airline-affiliated card programs limit the amount of charges that get mileage credit to $50,000 or so a year.

• *Two-for-one flights around the country.* Several of the airline cards offer a two-for-one voucher (which could be worth several hundred dollars to you) if you apply and are accepted for their card as an incentive to apply. The American Airlines program has done this fairly often. Generally, the offer is made to new members of the airline's frequent-flier club (membership is free simply by filling out an application for the club) by mail in the welcome package sent to new members. So on joining an airline's club, you may well get such a two-for-one voucher offer. But what about after you use that voucher to take your significant other to San Diego? You can negotiate with the credit card company for another voucher or an annual fee waiver when renewal time rolls around, especially if you fly a lot on the affiliated airline and also make big charges on the card. When the annual fee appears on your statement, just call up customer service, tell them you are thinking about canceling the card, and ask if they will waive it. Often they will, year after year. Or they will offer you another two-for-one flight voucher to get you to pay the annual fee and stay a member. Sometimes it helps to mention that you know of folks who got a new voucher by canceling the card and reapplying. Say to the service representative: "Why put the company and yourself to the trouble?" If you don't get what you want, there is nothing keeping you from switching to another airline's frequent-flier card. A good source of up-to-date information on these programs and current bonuses is *Best Fares Magazine* in Arlington, TX (800-880-1234, www.bestfares.com).

• *Free merchandise.* Many cards, especially around the winter holidays, offer merchandise bonuses in special seasonal mailings to cardholders. I recently got a truly lovely set of crystal champagne flutes from one kindly bank for making $300 in charges on its card in December. And one card company promised to send me two free movie tickets for making nine charges in January. Who knows what the mail might bring next holiday season?

• *Everything is negotiable.* Keep in mind that card companies spend lots of money to find new cardholders. If you arc a desirable card holder (i.e., one who pays the bills and charges up a storm), they don't want to lose you. Interest rate too high? Call customer service and ask them to cut the rate. Charged a late fee or a fee for a bounced check, perhaps because the mail was slow? Ask that it be waived. You lose nothing by asking. Very often you'll win.

*Financial Organization.* A plus of credit cards (and in some ways the reverse of the privacy problems they bring) is that they can help you organize your business and personal finances. If you charge everything you possibly can, you will have an almost complete record, along with your checking account register, of where your money went. This can be invaluable at tax time. One businesswoman told me: "I charge everything on one credit card, keep the monthly statements, and get a categorized summary of my purchases from the card company at the end of the year [a service available on some premium cards]. This really helps me be organized, something I have to be now that I have my own business. Plus, I get frequent-flier miles on what I charge." So credit cards can be exceedingly useful to you in organizing your finances. (And it's certainly nice to get those frequent-flier miles, which can add up to a free flight to Paris.)

*Personal Safety.* Credit cards may reduce the incentive for muggers. After all, if folks don't carry cash, why mug them? In fact someday you may not have a choice.

Consider Scan International Furniture of Rockville, Maryland, which recently introduced a no-cash policy at its stores. The stated reason was to stop robberies, and according to Russ Daily, Scan's president, in *HFN* (*Home Furnishing News*), the no-cash plan is doing what it is supposed to do. Daily says that only about 15 percent of the stores' sales were in cash and that he figured that most folks who paid in cash would change to checks or credit cards. Scan delivery drivers won't take cash either.

If a customer wants to pay with a money order, Scan pays for the money order; or if the item is less than $20 and the customer doesn't have a check or credit card with him or her, the clerk hands over the furniture polish or whatever, takes the customer's name and address, gives him or her a stamped, self-addressed envelope, and tells the customer to send in the payment. Daily says that every single person has mailed in the payment.

If this no-cash, mandatory payment by check or credit card idea catches on, it may cut back on crime at stores that adopt it but it will certainly hurt your privacy rights. You may not care if you have to let the bank know that you buy Scandinavian-designed furniture, but you might really care about letting the bank (and anybody who cares to look into its computer, with or without your permission) that you bought, say, *The Really Filthy Foot Fetish Picture Book* at the bookstore that refuses your anonymous cash. This is a trend that probably shouldn't catch on. Preventing crime is no doubt good, but so is protecting privacy; and if we lose our privacy at the furniture store, how soon before we lose it at the bookstore?

Credit cards have other advantages too.

• *They prevent airport security hassles.* Using a credit card to buy an airline ticket may keep you from being harassed at the airport. The

Federal Aviation Authority and the airlines have decided that if you buy a ticket with a check or cash you are more likely to be involved in illegal activity than if you pay with a credit card. Check- or cash-paying customers are more likely to be asked for additional information when they check in. Given that this tidbit has been published in the press, one might wonder how effective this distinction between passengers paying with credit cards and those who do not still is, but apparently it is still in effect.

• *They protect you against bankrupt airlines.* Charging airline tickets gives you good protection against airlines that go broke after you buy your ticket but before you fly. If you paid by cash or by check for that now-worthless ticket you would probably be out the money. If you charged it, you would probably be able to get your money back from the card company. I spoke to one lady who told me that she recovered over $800 through American Express when an airline went under.

*Stop-Payment Rights.* Perhaps the biggest advantage of using a credit card is your stop-payment rights, discussed in Chapter 11 of this book. Those rights can help keep you from being stung on many sorts of purchases. A good example is when you buy things by mail or phone order. It's very hard to understand why anyone who has a credit card would use anything else for a mail-order purchase because, when you use a credit card, unlike a check, if you don't get what you ordered you can stop payment on the charge and get your money back.

*Improved Credit Rating.* Another plus of using credit cards, so long as you make all your payments on time, is that regular use will help your credit rating by showing that you meet your credit commitments in timely fashion. Of course, if you don't meet those credit card commitments in timely fashion, your credit rating is hurt.

*Fewer Bank Trips.* Using a credit card can really cut down on those annoying trips to the bank to get cash. It's also great to be able to get a cash advance when the weekend looms and you're not in the vicinity of the bank that has your checking account.

*Extended Warranty, Theft, and Damage Protection.* Many cards provide theft, damage, and added warranty protection on purchases made with the card. These programs provide valuable benefits which many of us forget about when they might come in handy. When that home computer breaks down two weeks after the manufacturer's warranty expires, the free warranty on the credit card purchase will probably pay for the repairs if you have the original receipt. These warranty and theft protection programs require that you *closely* follow their some-times rather complex rules. I know of one fellow who left his new Burberry coat on a train in Belgium. The card he had charged the ticket on eventually paid for a new coat, but only after he had obtained a lost and found report (in French) from the railway police office in Brussels and an estimate of the replacement cost from Burberry's headquarters in London, all of which took a lot of time from his home in the Midwest.

*Ability to Purchase Bargains.* If you come across some super bargain in, say, a couch, or a trip to Paris, you can use your card to snap it up without worrying if your check is going to bounce.

*Float.* Things can cost you less when you pay by credit card. Float is the use of money you already spent before you pay the charge bill. Here you gain by not having to pay for purchases right away. You can put that money to use earning interest for you until it's needed to pay the bill.

## Kinds of Credit Cards

### Store Cards

As solid, steady growth continues to elude most of the nation's big merchants, many are aiming to enhance shoppers' purchasing power by offering new credit cards bearing their names. . . .

"Retail executives are just starting to realize how powerful the data they capture with their credit cards is," [partner and head of re-tail consulting at Manhattan management consultant McKinsey & Co.] Graham added: "The marketing potential should be perceived as the true value of the cards."

—Valerie Seckler in *HFN*
[*Home Furnishing News*]

Lots of stores—department stores, auto supply stores, computer stores, chain stores, gasoline companies—have their own credit cards. They have them for three main reasons:

1. Credit cards help sales. Traditionally stores make their money by selling their wares. Many studies have shown that people spend more money at stores where they have store-issued cards.
2. Stores make good money by financing their customers' purchases at high interest rates. In fact, many stores report making more money on their credit card operations than on sales of merchandise.
3. The stores have started to data-mine the very valuable information they can get from looking at the record of what you buy.

*Advantages of Store Cards.* Store cards certainly aren't all bad. Aside from the usually very high interest rate, they do offer you several pluses.

• They are easy credit cards to get. Even the cards of the prestige stores such as Saks, Nordstrom's, or Neiman Marcus are not so difficult to come by. In fact, the classy store cards are often much easier to get than less prestigious cards. Sears and JCPenney are reputed to be tougher than Neiman Marcus, for example.

The gasoline company cards are said to be the easiest of all cards to get. The gas companies want you to buy at their stations. They think you are more likely to pull up to their pumps if you have their card in your wallet. The old-fashioned oil company card, now being phased out by some companies, has no annual fee, charges a pretty high annual interest rate of around 18 percent, and has a very low credit limit—say, $300 or $500. Such an oil card can be used only at gas stations selling a certain brand of gas. But today, some newfangled oil cards can be used to charge airfares, meals, and hotel rooms. The oil companies have decided there is a lot of money to be made in the charge-it business. So the oil cards are looking more and more like bank cards—usable in many places. In fact, some oil companies have set up banks just to issue combination oil card/bank cards. Other store cards may try to make the jump to combination cards in the near future.

Stores know that if you have their card you are more likely to shop with them and are likely to spend more than you would if you had to take cash dollars out of your wallet. So they gladly pass out cards to anyone who looks as though they might be able to pay the bill.

• Store card customers can get preferred treatment. I talked to a gentleman who told me that when he went to an expensive store on Rodeo Drive in Beverly Hills to return a pair of shorts he was at first told it was too late for them to be taken back because "the season is over." When he said, "you can just credit it to my store charge account," the salesperson said, "Oh! You are one of our charge customers." And he returned the shorts with no more problems.

• Store cards give you extra leverage in getting problems with merchandise corrected. The store does not want to upset its best customers. And its assumption is that its best customers have, and use, the store's card.

• Stores often send cardholders, as their best customers, special catalogs and early notices of sales. There are more and more special "frequent charger" programs for store card or hybrid store/bank cardholders that provide extra discounts, free items, or a special bonus for purchases made with the store card.

• Finally, store cards provide somewhat greater stop-payment protection than do bank and T&E cards. The $50 and 100-mile limitations discussed in Chapter 10 do not apply to store cards.

*Disadvantages of Store Cards.* A very serious disadvantage is that store cards tend to carry interest rates higher than those of most other cards. Once upon a time, store accounts almost never charged interest. Some of the better, or at least more costly, stores did not even send a bill until months after a purchase was made. It is not like that anymore. Now the bills go out every month. There is a twenty- or thirty-day free-ride period when no interest is charged. If the bill is not paid off during that period, very high interest charges are added on by the company. In fact, some store cards don't even offer a grace or free-ride period. One company solicits consumers for a card that socks the card user for interest, even if the cardholder pays the account off in full as soon as the bill comes.

It used to be if you missed a payment or did not pay a bill on a store card it sometimes took a long, long time before the store reported you as a "slow pay" or "no pay" to the credit bureau, if they ever did. (Brooks Brothers used to be famous for this, they didn't even like to send out bills to their genteel clientele, it was said. But, things have changed at Brooksies). Many stores didn't wish to rile their best customers; they thought of credit as a service to their customers, not a profit center. Unfortunately, stores changed their ways as credit cards were made available to the hoi polloi. Today the store card is most definitely a profit center.

Today, if you do not pay off your balance in full each month the interest charges may be even higher than they would have been if you had used a bank or T&E card for your purchases. Be aware that store cards are often not the cheapest option for financing a purchase.

As *Consumer Action News* of San Francisco put it in a pre-Christmas story, "High Interest on Store Cards Can Haunt Holiday Shoppers All Year Long." Consumer Action said it surveyed sixty-two department and chain stores nationwide and found annual percentage rates on store cards as high as 22.9 percent—with 97 percent of the surveyed cards having an interest rate of 19.8 percent or higher. Ken McEldowny, director of the organization says: "If you want to use credit to pay for some of your holiday expenses, you are probably much better off using your [lower interest rate] bank credit card."

Scott Harshbarger, Massachusetts attorney general, says he is shocked and outraged by the rates charged on store cards: "There is an element of greed that I see here." Pete Willison, a consultant to credit card companies, says that rather than lower their rates around the holidays, retailers are more likely to raise credit limits and offer such things as "90 days, no interest" promotions.

Some stores are apparently so embarrassed over their rip-off interest rates that they don't want to disclose them on the application. For example, Consumer Action reported that cards used by a group of sister stores, including The Limited and Lane Bryant, which are issued by World Financial Network Bank of Ohio (a bank apparently owned by the stores), were charging interest rates as high as 22.8 percent, but that they took advantage of a complex and little-known loophole in federal law, which mostly requires up-front disclosure of interest rates and fees on the application, to avoid telling all on the application. Instead they say that you can call a toll-free number to "request specific information about such costs." Then when CA called the number, the first thing asked for by the automated system was your account number. How someone with no account number (or even someone *with* an account number) could squeeze information about interest rates out of the computerized system is unclear. And maybe that's the whole idea.

Yet another store card scam is the "zero interest" routine. With most of these offers ("No Interest Payments—Zero Percent Financing Until Halloween in the Year 2099!") interest is building up every day on the balance. If you pay the *entire amount* off *in full* before the zero percent deadline, the interest is "forgiven." Miss the deadline by thirty seconds and you'll be paying all the interest you thought you had avoided—and usually at an exorbitant interest rate like 22.8 percent too.

There is also the extra temptation to spend that all those cards make it oh-so-easy to give in to. But the temptation is more or less held in check because store cards are good in only a relatively few places. The new dual store cards, of course, have unlimited temptation, just like a regular bank-issued card. And many merchants find that the average sale on new store cards runs high. A clothing retailer headquartered in Florida says that sales on its newly issued store cards ran 30 percent higher than the average charge on American Express and 60 percent higher than the average sale at its stores.

Finally, there is the privacy issue store cards can present. Data mining lets the store know all sorts of private things about you. For example, you might buy maternity clothes at a store using your store card, and nine months later the chain might send you a baby clothes solicitation. If you used a Visa card to buy the maternity clothes, the store couldn't do that because it probably wouldn't be able to match up the dress sale with your address. Merchants theoretically can't usually get your address or telephone when you pay with a non-store card. They know only the account number and the name on the card. Of course, there *are* companies who will take a list of card numbers and names and reverse-match or reverse-append them to addresses and phone numbers from other credit applications, voter registration records, driver's license information, etc. No doubt some information entrepreneur will, absent emergency legislation, be selling this sort of stuff over the Internet.

American Express has been doing this sort of thing for a long time and also offers this sort of service to merchants. Buy a diamond necklace at a Beverly Hills store, and three weeks later you'll get an unasked-for call kindly advising you that the matching earrings have arrived. Let's just hope that when your spouse answers the call, that it was your spouse who got the necklace!

In fact, *The Wall Street Journal* reports that one major national casino operator has computerized information on six million people, including information on purchases made elsewhere that it buys from card companies and uses for targeted marketing to increase gambling by those in its database.

This sort of privacy invasion is building up quickly, and it looks as though some remarkable feats of tracking your personal information through your purchase history are well on the way. That's good if you're a hard marketing merchant; maybe not so good if you're a privacy-hungry consumer who already gets too many junk phone calls and way too much junk mail.

### The Dual Store/Bank Card

One reason that store cards may not be as gentle and kind as they once were is that cards issued directly by the merchant are being replaced by cards bearing the store's name, but actually issued by, say, XYZ National Bank. One of the most important reasons for the change is that under federal banking law, a store that issues its own card directly can be subject to strict state consumer protection laws regulating things such as interest rates and late fees. But a bank in another state, issuing a card that looks just like the old store card, right down to the trademarked store name on it, can ignore those pesky state laws. This practice boosts the store's profit margins as it costs you higher interest and late fees.

The name for this latest trend in store cards is dualing. A dual card has dual functions. *Bloomingdale's* is in big letters at the top of the card, but *Premier Visa* is written in smaller letters and the card bears a Visa logo. If you use it at Bloomingdale's, the next month you'll get a bill from Bloomingdale's, and Bloomingdale's can track your purchase information and send you a pillow solicitation after you buy a bed and two sets of those lovely flannel sheets with the zebra stripes they sell. If you use it to buy a ticket to New York at the Southwest Airlines ticket counter, Bloomingdale's doesn't find out about your ticket, and the bill arrives in a separate envelope from FDS National Bank, located in Mason, Ohio. A dual card is both a store card and a bank card.

As Bloomingdale's puts it:

> Your Bloomingdale's Premier Visa is more powerful than other store cards because it is a Bloomingdale's Card with the added benefits of a Visa Card . . .
>
> * Two separate credit lines, one at Bloomingdale's and one with Visa
> * Two separate statements, one for each card account
> * Worldwide acceptance of Visa.

Use of the dual store/bank card means you are no longer covered by your state's consumer protection laws on such things as overlimit fees and bounced check charges. The dual card generally has a credit limit much higher than that of a store card, and this may adversely affect your ability to get other credit, such as a home mortgage, by showing up as a high potential loan on your credit report. Dual type cards are not necessarily bad, but when you are offered one (usually in a letter that says something like "Because of your excellent record, you have been chosen for a special new Widget Store/MasterCard," be sure you know what you are getting into before you accept. You have no obligation to accept the offer, whatever form it's made in, (your permission is required to issue this new dual card, although the offer may not tell you this). You can simply not accept it and keep your old, non-dual card, should you so choose.

### Bank Cards

Bank cards are the most common and useful credit cards. Visa and MasterCard are the two most common bank cards. To get a Visa or MasterCard you must deal with a financial institution that is a *member* of the Visa or MasterCard organizations. While Visa and Master-Card are called bank cards, you can get them from savings and loan associations, credit unions, and several other sorts of organizations. Initially the cards were called bank cards because they came only from banks. The name has stuck.

You get a bank card from an issuing bank or other organization. You can *never* get a card from the Visa or MasterCard organizations. They handle many of the operations that make the bank card systems run. But they do not issue cards. Visa and MasterCard started out as sort of co-ops run by bankers for their mutual benefit, but now they are so successful, big, and powerful that some think they may, at times, be pushing around the members who purportedly run the credit card show, especially the smaller members.

Each financial institution sets its own terms for the cards it issues. Two Visa cards may look exactly alike, but be very different in cost and in the benefits that come with them. The Visa card from Bank A may have a $40 annual fee, carry a 21 percent annual interest rate and a 3 percent cash advance fee, and have a grace period of only fifteen days after you are billed for making payments before you have to pay interest. Bank B's Visa card might have no annual fee, a 12 percent annual interest rate, no cash advance fee, and a grace period of twenty-five days. They both say VISA in big letters. But Bank B's card is a much better deal. The key point to remember about Visa and Master-Card plastic is that each bank sets the charges for using the cards it puts out, so one Visa card may have terms very different from those of a Visa card issued by another bank. The same is true of benefits and services. One MasterCard may offer special insurance for car rentals paid for with that card while a MasterCard from another bank may have no such insurance. You have to check each card out individually.

So you must shop for the best possible price and terms on your bank card. Unfortunately, the financial institutions that issue cards don't make shopping easy. In fact, they go out of their way to make it difficult. Card marketers today often emphasize unimportant features, such as the purported prestige of the platinum card, or make claims like: "Call us twenty-four hours a day" or "Credit limit increase requests responded to within ten minutes." Much more important are the fees and interest charges associated with the card. These are usually not featured in advertising or direct mail solicitations, or if they are, one low charge is featured without any more than the minimal, legally required mention of other important charges. Advertising is not usually a good guide to the value of a card.

✍

The Discover card put out by Dean Witter, Discover & Company (founder Sears sold out years ago) is a kind of bank card, although Discover uses a maze of different companies (such as Novus Services, Inc.) to run the Discover card business. You can use a Discover card at Sears and at lots and lots of other stores, although not quite so many as Visa or MasterCard. But the Discover card has gone a long way toward being as widely accepted as the other cards.

Right now, only Discover issues Discover cards. And right now, there is no annual fee for the Discover card. Discover has pointedly made no promises about not charging annual fees in the future and has started selling "Private Issue" cards that do have an annual fee. In my opinion, Discover has a history of charging very high interest rates and of using expensive, anti-consumer methods of computing interest rates. Discover has also sent out thousands of "preapproved" card solicitations and then refused to honor those "preapproved" offers, claiming "computer error."

*Advantages of Bank Cards.* The big advantage of bank cards is their very wide acceptance. Visa and MasterCard can be used at more stores and banks in the United States and abroad than any other kind of card, mostly because it costs the merchant less to take a Visa or MasterCard than to take cards such as American Express or Diners, which usually charge the merchant a much higher commission.

The annual bank card fee is usually much lower than that charged by the T&E cards, or there may be no annual fee. In fact, the only bank card you may need to pay a fee for is one that offers a big, valuable extra, generally frequent-flier miles or some other sort of bonus. Almost all the airlines have an affiliated bank-issued Visa or MasterCard program (Delta's is an Optima card from American Express, which, because it lets cardholders carry a balance, is closer to a bank card than a T&E card) that lets you get frequent-flier miles for every dollar charged. Run up 25,000 miles and you can take a free flight in the continental United States. Rack up lots more miles and you may get a free trip to Europe, depending on the airline. Obviously these cards are good deals if you run a lot of money through your account and pay off the balance every month (thus avoiding the very high interest charges of most of these cards), getting bonus miles for every charge. They're not so good if you don't charge so much because you may never get enough miles for a free trip before the miles expire (after three years under many of the airline programs).

Bank cards can also be used to get a cash advance (that means loan) at many banks around the world, but beware the many possible hidden costs—for example, the notorious cash advance fee and instantly accruing interest. Fortunately there are a few cards without such a fee; check *Money* or some other personal finance magazine for possibilities or use the Internet resources discussed in Chapter 15. Card issuer

USAA Federal Savings Bank (800-922-9092) has a good history of not charging cash advance fees.

With a bank card, because they are accepted in so many places, you can charge almost everything you buy and benefit from playing the float (float is the use of money you get when you borrow and don't have to pay interest for a period). You can pay for everything with one check, rather than writing out many checks. You also benefit from having all your purchases listed and totaled for you. This can be a great convenience for your record-keeping and to help you keep track of things for tax and other reasons. And the statements provide proof of purchase and of the date of purchase for warranty purposes.

*Disadvantages of Bank Cards.* First, for some bank cards, you must pay an annual fee. Happily this is the *one* bank card fee which is disappearing (frequent-flier cards are the exception here; they have kept annual fees), due to changes in the industry brought on by the AT&T Universal Card and others who in the early 1990s started promoting "no annual fee" and "no annual fee for life" as a way to win over card users to their new card programs and to induce them to transfer those profitable, interest-generating balances from other cards.

Second, exactly because bank cards are so widely accepted and therefore so useful, they can be very dangerous. You can end up charging all sorts of things you ultimately cannot pay for—and at all kinds of places. So can a crook who finds a way to access your account. That is trouble!

Third, bank card customer service tends to be several notches down from that of travel and entertainment cards (discussed below) and at least some store cards. If you have a simple problem with a bank card, such as a billing error overcharge for a hotel room in Las Vegas, it may be more difficult to get it resolved than it would be with, say, a T&E or store card. (Not that T&E, store, or bank cards win big prizes for solving even slightly complex problems.)

Fourth, interest rates on bank cards can be, and mostly are, unreasonably high. Banks are making huge profits from super-high interest charges on card accounts. They are not inclined to change their ways. Congress has looked into the problem, but so far, the political clout of the banks has kept any controls on rip-off card interest rates from passage.

Fifth, fees other than annual fees, many of which are rather complex and hidden (late fees, overlimit fees, bad check fees, statement copy fees), lurk in the shadows waiting to jump out and bite the unwary bank card user. The banks won a huge victory in the 1996 Supreme Court case of *Smiley v. Citibank* (116 S.Ct. 1730); according to the decision in this case, an out-of-state bank can evade many of the consumer protection laws of the cardholder's home state. Congress should really address this issue with a change in the law. Why should a bank in, say, South Dakota be allowed to charge a $35 late payment fee to someone who lives in another state, a state whose laws limit late payment fees to $5? There is no good reason. But now you know why banks are running to notoriously anticonsumer states such as South Dakota and Delaware to set up subsidiary banks that actually issue their cards. For example, if you have a card from Citibank, it probably does not come from New York, where Citibank is headquartered, but from Citibank (South Dakota), a special credit card bank in that state.

### Travel and Entertainment Cards

Today you can use travel and entertainment (T&E) cards, which include the American Express, Carte Blanche, and Diners Club cards, for lots more than travel or entertainment. Back in ancient days (the fifties) T&E cards could be used only for eating out and charging hotel and travel expenses. Today all sorts of stores take these cards, but the old name lives on.

Two important differences between T&E cards and other credit cards are:

1. T&E cards let you have only very short-term credit. The longest period of credit you can get with the most common T&E cards is just under two months.
2. You are not charged direct interest on the credit you do get from them.

Don't worry about the T&E companies, though; they have other ways of making out.

With T&E cards you theoretically must pay up within thirty or so days of the time you get your bill. So the most time you can have before you must pay for something you charge on a T&E card is just under two months. You get that much time if you charge something the day after billing closes for the month. For example, you charge something on May 1, assuming the credit card company closes its statements on the last day of each month. The May 1 charge will not be billed to you until May 31 and you will be in good standing even if you don't pay until the last day of June. This is the same way the free-ride period works with cards that let you extend your payments over a longer time.

There are ways to legitimately extend your payments for a longer time, but they involve special programs and are not a part of the standard features of T&E cards. Paying under these special programs will also have you paying interest. The American Express Optima card is an example of one such program.

The T&E card companies have three ways of making the most of their money. First, they charge you a hefty annual fee, from $55 on up. The T&E annual fee is really an interest charge, one that is very high when you do not charge a lot. The fee stays the same no matter how much you charge with a T&E card.

Second, they charge the merchants a remarkably large percentage of any purchase made on the card, up to 10 percent of the sale. This is much more than any other type of card charges the merchant. These rates have dropped a bit as the T&Eers have sought to extend merchant acceptance of their cards.

Third, they do not pay the merchants immediately, sometimes playing the float, holding the merchants' money for up to thirty days.

*Advantages of T&E Cards.* Prestige is the big advantage of these cards—that is, if you are into prestige and if you really believe that a piece of plastic can make you a more loved person. The T&E companies spend millions to convince us that paying the bar tab with their card will cause the world to look on us more favorably. Unfortunately, this doesn't look to be true. Where I come from, just paying the bar tab makes the world look on you most favorably. The form of payment is your business.

Other T&E card advantages are maybe a little more real than prestige.

- "Country club" billing, where you get a copy of the actual charge slip you signed at the store instead of a computer printout of what the credit card companies claim you have to pay. However, Diners just eliminated this, and American Express sends computer-printed copies of the slips rather than the originals.

• A somewhat better level of service. On the average, T&E customer contact folks seem to be a little more on the ball than folks at the banks. (This is not such high praise, but it is praise).

• Toll-free 800 numbers to call up with your billing problems. The only problem is that calling will not protect your credit card user rights. For that you have to send a letter (see Chapter 8). So if you use the 800 number and things do not get fixed, you are out of luck, legally speaking.

• Special services to card users when they travel. American Express appears to really deliver on this. It will cash checks, hold mail, and re-place lost or stolen cards *fast* (seven minutes is the record so far as I know, with overnight par for the course) for Amexco card users in the United States and abroad. Do not expect this kind of action from a bank card or from the other T&E cards.

• No preset spending limit. That means that they do not have a fixed credit limit of, say, $2,500, as a bank card does. *Note that no preset spending limit does not mean no limit.* Your charging patterns are monitored by the T&E company. If there is a big change in your pattern of spending or if your charges start to get outside the area that the company thinks you can pay back, you will find your leash quickly yanked.

Say one dreary winter month you decide to take off, leave your job as auditor for the North Alaska Pipeline and Trapping Corporation, and live it up in Key West, Florida, first class all the way. Before you get up to the first $10,000 in charges, American Express will be con-tacting you to inquire (politely at first) if someone has stolen your card. Or to ask just why you are charging $900 a day instead of your usual average of $12.43.

No preset limit does *not* mean no limit. No matter what the T&E card folks try to imply.

*Disadvantages of T&E Cards.* First, of course, is the hefty annual fee.

Second is the inability to extend payments in an emergency without a big hassle. You can negotiate extended payments with a T&E com-pany if you can think of a reason the company likes. It is not too diffi-cult if you have a previously good payment record. But with a bank card you have the *right* to extend payment, which can be a fine thing if you have good self-control. Some folks do like the financial discipline that the "pay it all every month" T&E card forces on them.

Third, you may get a not-so-great foreign exchange rate with T&E cards when they are used abroad, although the bank cards are catching up with the T&E cards on this by raising costs on foreign charges.

Fourth, you cannot use T&E cards at nearly as many places as you can use bank cards. Mostly, you are limited to the more expensive shops and restaurants. Discount retailers rarely take T&E cards. They cannot afford to pay the steep commission the T&E companies would charge them. For example, the remarkable 99 Cents Only stores of Southern California take only MasterCard and Visa. The manager of one such store told me that they had looked into accepting other cards, but it was just too costly for them.

Fifth, it may be difficult and costly to get a cash advance on a T&E card. Often it is impossible. You can cash checks at T&E company offices around the world (if you can find one, which, except for American Express, may be difficult) but you cannot get actual cash on the card itself. Diners does let you get cash on your card, but charges *very* steep fees. And it has a limited number of affiliated offices where you can actually get cash.

Sixth, the number of T&E offices is limited. American Express has by far the most around the world, but even it comes nowhere near matching the number of banks at which a bank-type credit card can be used for, say, cash advances. But I admit, if I'm going to have my card stolen in Milan, Italy, I'd probably get a new card a lot faster from American Express than I would from the First National Bank of Buncum.

## *Gold Cards and Platinum Cards*

QUESTION: "What is the difference between a Green Card and a Gold Card?"

ANSWER: "The difference is that the Green Card is green and the Gold Card is gold, and if you don't understand that, then you don't understand this company."

—attributed to Aldo Papone, chairman of
American Express Travel-Related Services Division

Percent of millionaires with an American Express Platinum Card: 6.2.

Percent of millionaires with a Sears credit card: 43.

SOURCE: *Smart Money* magazine

There's been a big change in the marketing of Technicolor credit cards in the last few years. Originally, gold cards were held up as something special for the elite (read *well-to-do*), and they were more difficult to get, with credit limits of at least $5,000 and special services not available on the tawdry regular credit card level. But that's all different now. Gold cards are available to almost anyone; credit limits of $5,000 or much more are readily available on regular, non-gold cards. And the special features on gold cards have been cut back in many cases and are now often just as available on the regular cards. At present the card companies are battling for the name "platinum card," which they think will open up new vistas of marketing and exploitation. Some companies are even working on the next level, the "titanium card."

We've all seen those ads for metallic-colored plastic cards: gold, platinum, silver, and whatever. The ads promise that if you carry one of these super-prestige pieces of plastic that headwaiters in fancy French restaurants and members of the opposite sex will collapse gasping at your feet just at the sight of that tiny piece of plastic. Seems rather unlikely, doesn't it?

But the card folks have got to have some way to justify the extra $30 to $300 and more that many will sock you for if you can be convinced that you must have one of their specially colored goodies. They have to sell you something you can't see, hear, smell, touch, or feel— like nonexistent prestige. The vaunted advantages of the special cards, in general, don't really exist. Indeed, the advantages of the metallic cards are so elusive today that most of the companies issuing them have dropped their annual fees and hope to make their money in other ways.

In fact, the high gold card credit limit can really be a trap. Why pay 20 percent interest on $5,000 or $10,000 of charges when you can get a regular loan for half that rate? It's silly. But people do it.

Consider that cash advances average four times larger on goldie Visa and MasterCard accounts than on regular bank card accounts. The goldie folks don't usually get any special break. They pay the same hefty charges for cash advances that the normal bank card user gets stuck for.

Finally, a gold card may make you more likely to be a victim of fraud. Since a gold Visa or MasterCard generally has a credit limit of at least $5,000, many organized card fraud rings look for gold cards to use in scams because the higher credit limits make it more profitable.

What do you really get from the "prestige" cards? Not much. And mostly not enough to justify any extra charge.

But there are occasionally some extra goodies with a metallic card:

• *Rental-car insurance.* Some card companies offer insurance to cover the collision damage waiver that car rental companies now use to rip off their customers. This policy, which covers you if you charge the car rental on many gold cards, is a valuable benefit, one that does not cost you the ten or fifteen or twenty dollars a day the rent-a-car folks want for much the same coverage. But many regular, non-gold cards offer the same coverage today. You have to read the papers the card company sends about insurance coverage or call the company and ask to find out. Anyway, the best deal around on such coverage is, in my opinion, that offered by the Diners (ungold) card. Diners card coverage is primary, not secondary, which means that if, God forbid, you have a crash in a rental car, Diners will pay the rental company for the damage without first making you go to your own insurer and make a claim. Most other companies cover you only for what your insurer won't pay. So if you have personal auto insurance, it probably also covers you for most of the damage you might do to a rental car, but the card company (if it's not Diners) will probably insist that you make a claim with your own insurance company and will cover only what your company won't pay.

Note that there are changes afoot here. MasterCard and Visa have cut back on their coverage on many non-gold cards and American Express has eliminated coverage for some countries where it says the claims have been too expensive, such as Italy, Israel, Ireland, and Jamaica. Call the bank that issues a card you are thinking about using to rent a car abroad and ask what the current coverage is. Ask that a written statement of the coverage be sent to you and put it in your file.

• *Lower interest rates.* Some gold bank cards do carry an interest rate lower than that of the normal card from the same issuer. This could be worthwhile if you carry a large balance on your card and if you are unable to find a normal card with an even lower interest rate, which shouldn't be to hard too do today.

• *Referrals.* The gold bank cards, Diners, and Amex provide free referrals for medical and legal services most places in the world. A free referral doesn't mean you won't get charged by the doctor or whomever you're referred to.

My advice? Ignore the card's color. Judge a card by its interest, fees, and services. The sole exception, the American Express Platinum Card, comes loaded with extras. You can get special opera tickets and two-for-one deals on business-class flights to Europe and on the supersonic Concorde. If this sort of thing is important to you and you don't mind the current $300 (!) annual fee, why then, go ahead and apply. (American Express claims you have to be *invited* to apply for the card, but I suspect that if you call Amex customer service and ask, you may well get an application.)

Interestingly, American Express, having lost a legal battle for the exclusive use of the term Gold Card, is now fighting with several banks over the right to use of Platinum Card. At least two banks decided to try to move up-market with platinum-colored cards with up to $100,000 credit limits (Gosh, Ma, I got to have that ermine tipped solid diamond cape right now today—and it's only $99,999.99!). The

---

**• CREDIT CARD INSIDER'S TIP •**

*Never* pay a credit card fee up front, before the account is opened. Any company you want to do business with will charge any fee to your new account after it's opened. If they want you to pay *anything* up front, they probably think you won't want to pay after you see what they are *really* selling.

---

banks don't offer the same level of special services that American Express does, but they don't charge a $300 annual fee either; in fact they issue their platinum cards at no annual fee. And I've heard from holders of American Express Platinum Cards that Amexco has cut back a bit on its services to them—for example, eliminating a travel service that gave holders of that sacred card certain travel services not available to those worthy of merely moderate credit.

*Scam "Gold" Cards.* A popular scam is marketing phony "gold" cards good for buying only overpriced items from only one catalog. These are usually offered to folks who are in some sort of credit difficulties. Often tied in with some purported membership in a special buyers' club, the junk mail package tries very hard to look like it is offering you a Visa or MasterCard gold card. It may even have the Visa and MasterCard logos prominently displayed on the envelope and order blank. But that doesn't mean that it's a Visa or MasterCard you can use almost anywhere to buy almost anything. Instead, it may mean only that you can *use* a Visa or MasterCard to pay the exorbitant annual fee that the fake gold card company wants to sell you. The typical scam indicates that signing up for the fake gold card will somehow help with your credit problem, but it won't.

# Big, Big Credit Card Profits:
# From Your Wallet
# to the Bank's Vault

> Given relatively high interest rates and fat margins the card business is still very profitable. Credit cards are having difficulties, charge-offs are up, personal bankruptcies are high, yet all these [credit card] companies are announcing record earnings.
> —John B. McCoy, chairman and CEO,
> Banc One Corporation, America's third largest card issuer

> The credit card is the most consequential product the U.S. banking industry has ever invented. If you look at the profitability over the last ten to fifteen years it clearly buoyed the bulk of the U.S. banking industry and was in fact the salvation of some of our largest banks.
> —Alex W. "Pete" Hart, former president,
> MasterCard, quoted in *American Banker*

Look at credit card company ads. They try to convey the impression that credit cards were invented only to provide wonderful, lovable you with super service and instant gratification of your every desire, be it worthy or unworthy.

This impression is wrong. While cards may or may not serve you conveniently and pleasurably, that is not the reason they exist.

Credit cards exist so the folks giving out the cards can make big bucks! There is big, *big, BIG* money to be made selling credit cards. In fact, conventional wisdom in the banking business says that the credit card business is three or four times more profitable than most of the banks' other business. Collecting 20 percent interest while paying out 1 percent on deposits is clearly a rather profitable business.

True, credit cards provide many valuable services to card users (albeit often at a very high cost). Indeed, I got my first credit card when I was working for the U.S. Senate Judiciary Committee back in the seventies because the super high rate of inflation back then made it a good idea to buy things right away, before the price went up. My shiny new card let me buy at the lower, less-inflated price even though I didn't have the cash.

Still, I'll never forget the credit card convention I went to where the featured speaker, a very high-ranking federal banking regulator, came out to the podium to loud applause, turned toward the audience, and applauded them back. He started his speech by saying that he and the entire banking industry should be applauding them as the people who ran the most profitable part of the banking business, a segment so profitable that it had helped cover the gigantic losses the banks had generated on overseas and real estate loans. Apparently he thought that high credit card interest rates and profits were a good thing—a good thing that helped bail many banks out of the losses from defaulted loans, a good thing that kept the government from having to cover those losses from bank insurance funds, which might not have been up to the task.

Profits are why all those stores hire people to pounce on customers at the door and hand out chocolate bars and digital watches to anyone who will fill out a credit card application. As one example, Sears gets about half of its profits from its in-house credit card operations. Profits are why you see card applications on every cigarette machine in America and why American Express, Diners, and zillions of banks pay $1.00 on up (way up) to merchants for each accepted application that a store's customers send in.

### Three Main Ways the Card Companies Make Big Money

The real enemy here is cash and checks.
—President Robert Seander of MasterCard International
in *The Wall Street Journal*

*The House Cut*
The card companies get a percentage of the price of everything paid for with credit cards. When you charge something, be it a restaurant meal, a silk shirt, or some Tums, the store gets to keep only around 90 to 98

percent of the amount you charge. The other 2 to 10 percent is kept by the card issuers as their slice. That is a pretty hefty cut for the card companies.

If you use a bank card, the bank whose name is on your card gets about half the withheld amount and the bank that the store has its account with gets the other half. A little something goes to the Visa or MasterCard association, depending on what kind of card you use.

If you use a T&E card, then American Express or Diners or Carte Blanche keep the whole hunk. And that hunk can go up to almost 10 percent of the amount you charge. T&E cards are generally lots more costly for the merchant than bank cards.

The credit card companies are well on their way to getting a profitable percentage of just about every purchase in the nation. That cut of every sale made on a credit card is the first way they make big bucks off you.

### Annual Fees (Thank You Jimmy Carter)

Another big (although fading) moneymaker for credit card companies is annual fees. T&E companies have long had annual fees, although the T&Eers have jacked them up considerably of late. Store cards do not charge them. Bank cards did not have them until 1979, the year that Jimmy Carter got the Federal Reserve Bank to put controls on how much money bankers could loan out to credit card users. The idea was that cutting down on consumer loans would cut down the then out-of-control inflation rate.

The new controls let bankers yank the leash on credit card customers. They eliminated what little price competition there had been between card companies. The banks immediately used the controls as an excuse to invent new and very profitable annual fees for each card and blamed it on the government. But they didn't feel obliged to give the money to the government. Instead they kept it (surprise!) and used the extra income to advertise for new card customers.

It was the annual fee that initiated the blitz of card applications that now afflict us. Any credit card marketer will tell you that. A $25 or $50 annual fee more than covers the cost to a bank of attracting a customer. Annual fees finance the ongoing credit card advertising wars along with newly jacked up and hard-to-defend fees such as overlimit and late fees. They also helped many of the card companies to aggressively start soliciting the poor.

When the banks tacked annual fees onto their cards, that made it possible for American Express and the other T&E cards to raise their annual fees. If the low-class bank cards were going to charge twenty-five bucks a year, by golly, the high-class T&E cards were going to get lots more than that!

---

I have very little sympathy for issuers that made deliberate business decisions to aggressively solicit high-risk customers, then saw their delinquency rates skyrocket later. In a sense, they *did* ask for it.
—John W. Milligan, editor in chief, *U.S. Banker,*
in a column entitled "Stupid Card Tricks"

---

Don't pay an annual fee unless you have to. Fortunately, you do not have to. There are many banks that issue cards and charge no annual fee. Yet they provide the same services as the other, costly banks' cards. *Get one of those no-fee cards!* (The only exception is when you get something extra for paying the extra fee—for example, the frequent-flier card that gives you points for free flights on one or more airlines for each dollar you charge.)

A variation on the annual fee scheme that a few banks use is a transaction fee. Each time you use a card, those banks tack 25¢ or so onto the amount you charge. This can quickly cost you more than an annual fee. Some might say that's why they do it. Fortunately, this routine seems to be dying out. It was too easy for consumers to understand that it was a rip-off.

Some banks take in more than 100 million dollars a year from annual fees alone. That pays for all those Citibank Visa applications that litter the pages of magazines that Citibank thinks are read by people who may be so foolish as to apply for one of the most expensive Visa cards in existence. It pays for all those applications that sit in four-color cardboard displays on store counters. And it pays for the junk mail applications that flood the mailboxes of those who live in a zip code area the credit card marketers think is full of affluent suckers.

Consumers owe no thanks to President Carter for raising the cost of credit to card users. But thanks are due for annual card fees to President Carter. From every credit card company in America.

Fortunately, annual fees appear to be slowly retreating. When the AT&T Universal Card was introduced in the early nineties, one of its big selling points was "no annual fee for life." Although even then there were many other, less publicized cards available with no annual fee, AT&T was just about the first really big issuer to push the idea of no annual fee so hard. The tidal wave from this move by AT&T has washed away many annual fees and has raised treacherous reefs of all sorts of other fees.

Annual fees are pretty easy to understand. Either you agree to pay one to get the card or you don't. The same is not true of the much more popular (with the card companies) overlimit fees, late fees, returned check fees, hasn't-paid-enough-interest-this-year fees, and so forth. Overlimit fees, late fees, and bounced check fees are especially beloved by card companies because folks often feel guilty for going over their credit limit, being late in making a payment, or bouncing a check, and customers who feel guilty are less likely to complain about the exorbitant fees charged by many companies for these minor (and not very costly to the companies) transgressions. If processing a bounced check costs 83¢ and the company can sock the check bouncer for a $25 fee, without getting complaints, that's a pretty good deal—for the company. Industry studies suggest that late fees and overlimit fees are very profitable indeed. Given that a cardholder who is late in paying or who goes over the assigned credit limit continues to be charged interest at a very high rate, these fees are questionable indeed.

### Socko Interest Rates

The third money maker (and the one the card companies may love the most) is the *remarkably* high interest that the companies charge on what you don't pay off during the free-ride period. There is no good reason for these very high interest rates. There's no good reason card users should pay 18 or 21 percent when the banks are borrowing money from savers at 1 or 2 percent. This huge spread lets those bankers make *unbelievable* profits. Most card companies could make good money paying 5 percent interest and getting 10 percent or even less from you in interest.

So far card companies have been able to get away with extraordinary interest charges because of the lack of any serious competition in the industry. Real competition in the credit card business is almost nonexistent. As Kate Griffin, contributing editor of *Credit Card Management*, wrote in an article entitled "The Antitrust Waiting Game": "Virtually everyone agrees that the birth of duality [the membership of banks in both the Visa and MasterCard associations] more than two decades ago meant the death of true competition between the bank card brands." And because consumers don't understand the many complexities the card companies have created to confuse consumers— complexities industry insiders are in no rush to explain.

*Pay Interest Every Month or They Get Mad.* If you *do* pay off your balance every month within the no-interest period, you are what the card companies call a free rider. Or in their nastier moments, freeloaders. Or at their nastiest, leeches.

Card companies hate free riders. Card company executives dream of the day when the free ride will be eliminated. Then, the card execs dream, they will make some *real* money. These executives seem to think that it is your *duty* to pay them lots of interest when you charge something. First, they told you that if you paid the bill off in twenty-five or thirty days, it would not cost you anything to charge. A free ride, they said. Now they get mad when you actually *do* pay off and don't pay interest.

*Super High Interest Means Super Big Profits.* There is plenty of profit for credit card companies in just the rake-off they get from stores and from annual fees alone, without any interest payments at all. American Express, which wants all its money every month, does rather well for itself, but it collects relatively little in interest money from Amex card users. No doubt Amexco would like to change that, and its introduction of the Optima card, which does allow the carryover of balances from month to month, is a way to move toward collection of more interest from cardholders.

"Consumers are getting slaughtered with these interest rates," says Neil Fogarty, president of the New Jersey Consumer League. The league wants the state of New Jersey to cut its permitted interest rate from 30 percent a year. That's a pretty sweet rate for the banks with inflation running at 3 or 4 percent a year. A lot of bankers say *they* sure would not borrow at the rates they charge. "It doesn't make sense to pay 19 or 20 percent for money when inflation is about 4 percent and you can only earn 7 or 8 percent on your savings," according to a big wheel economist at big-time Bankers' Trust of New York.

*The New York Times* says: "The continuing high rates . . . are beginning to raise questions about [interest rate] deregulation. Its advocates have argued that if usury laws [which regulate interest rates] were removed—and most have been—competition among financial institutions would keep rates relatively low." The *Times* is right when it says that most usury laws have been repealed or amended to make them ineffective. But the advocates of deregulation were wrong in their claim that deregulation of interest rates would keep those rates low. Just take a look at one of your recent credit card statements and see if the card company is charging a reasonable rate—say 8 or 9 percent. Chances are it's more than twice a reasonable rate, more like 18 or 20 percent.

Congressman Charles Schumer of New York City does not think that the free market system is working in the credit card world. Says he, "With so many banks and so much competition, why don't consumer rates follow the cost of money down?" Maybe there isn't any real competition.

---

**• CREDIT CARD INSIDER'S TIP •**

Think of paying off credit cards on which you are paying interest as the smartest money-management move you can make.

Pay off those big balances and put the interest in your pocket instead of the card company's. Since the corner bank is likely paying around 2 percent on savings accounts, you can do much better by paying off credit card bills with savings. Many folks would benefit by getting a low-rate loan from, say, a credit union and paying off their card balance in full with the loan.

---

## What's in It for the Merchants?

Why do stores and restaurants give up a hunk of their sales money to the banks and T&E companies? Why don't they simply say, "No, thanks, we won't accept your cards here. Then we won't have to pay you anything"? Many of the best restaurants in France and Sweden, places where people keep a close eye on their money, have boycotted American Express cards. The restaurant chefs said it was not possible to pay the high rake-off demanded by Amexco and still have enough money left over to pay the costs of a quality restaurant. Not unless the restaurant raised its already high prices, which wasn't practical. American Express defused the chefs' revolt by cutting its fees for the complainers.

Clearly, merchants think there is something in taking credit cards for them: bigger sales, which equal bigger profits for the merchants. That is what the merchants believe they get. Card companies have oodles of surveys and piles of studies that show that customers spend more money faster using credit cards. And they are right. Ask a waiter. He'll tell you that credit card users in general are bigger tippers, order more expensive meals, booze it up more, and are bigger sports, in the "light up my seegar with that hundred-dollar bill" tradition.

The department store manager will inform you that the per-purchase amount on credit card sales is bigger than the cash sales. And that with credit cards, there is lots more impulse buying. The small store owner will agree. Their opinions count, since they have the power to sign up their businesses with the credit card guys.

The merchants think they are making more money in total by taking credit cards than they would if they did not take cards. Even so, there is a constant battle between merchants and credit card companies about what the merchants must pay when they accept the cards. Every merchant pays a discount, some percentage of the total purchase, to the card company when the merchant takes a credit card. It may be 5 percent of the total purchase, it may be ½ of 1 percent of the total purchase. The discount is very negotiable, but many card companies don't like to let merchants, especially small merchants, know that. The more a card company can get in the discount, the higher its profits. And if a small merchant doesn't know to demand a lower, more reasonable discount rate, all the better for the card companies.

Some merchants, like the French chefs mentioned above, say they simply cannot pay what the card companies want from them and stay in business.

This is a problem for American restaurants too. Profit margins in the restaurant business are relatively low, and the cut the card companies take when a customer charges a meal is painful to the restaurant profits. Thus, around 100 of Boston's top restaurants threatened a boycott of American Express for charging around 3.5 percent of a bill put on an American Express Card. American Express apparently cut its rates to those restaurants. The famous Bern's Steak House in Tampa did drop American Express, saying the alternative was to raise prices.

The big stores are very conscious of what it costs them to accept plastic. In Los Angeles, Joanna Logsdon, general credit manager for Bullock's (now Macy's) department stores, said she compares prices from many banks for the very best deal. She does it every year to ensure that her stores are not paying more than they should.

---

### GROCERIES—CREDIT CARDS NOW ACCEPTED

A good example of the expansion of card use and the expansion of card company profits is the grocery business. Not so long ago you couldn't use cards at most grocery stores. The discount rake-off to the card companies was the reason you couldn't use a credit card to buy groceries except at the most costly places. The discount the credit card guys wanted from the food stores was more than the stores' average profit percentage on a sale. A grocery store couldn't take plastic without jacking up its prices 2 percent or more, and that would have priced most stores too much above the competition.

But the credit card folks didn't give up. Tempted by the vast dollar volume of grocery sales, the card companies worked like crazy to get a plastic foot in the food store door by pushing the Financial Death Card (that is to say, the debit card, which is discussed in Chapter 4) as a good way for merchants to increase sales at minimal cost. The card companies offered special very low discount rates on debit card purchases. The Financial Death Card, the cardies explained, would bring in new customers who might go elsewhere if debit cards were not accepted and would bring in these new customers at very low cost—even free if the cost of counting up the cash, which would be eliminated by computerization, was figured in. Then, having used the debit card to get in the grocery store door, the card companies maneuvered to get credit cards accepted at the food store. Credit cards were a little more expensive for the grocers to accept, but the introductory rates were still low. Then somehow those special, very low discount rates got higher and higher and higher. And now the card companies are collecting an ever-increasing portion of America's food dollar at an ever-increasing cost to shopping Americans. But the card companies are still very hungry indeed. I suspect they won't be happy until everything in the world is paid for with plastic and they collect a monopoly toll on each and every purchase, groceries and all.

The big guys know they have to shop credit card rates and know how to get the information to do so. Smaller merchants should be alert to the fact that what they pay to take credit cards is negotiable. The government should, but does not require the card companies to provide full information on the range of prices the companies charge to merchants so that smaller business have the information they need to bargain with the companies.

Fortunately, there is plenty you, the consumer, can do to cut the toll the card companies collect from you. Educate yourself by reading on, and save.

The consumer cannot shop easily for credit. Credit card companies have carefully hidden from him or her much of the shopping information the consumer needs. Or they have made such information very difficult to get and understand. Only rarely will a call to a card company connect you with someone willing or able to tell you about *all* the costs of the card. Without useful information from the seller, rational shopping is difficult, if not impossible.

3

# The Real Costs of Credit Cards— and How to Reduce Them

Credit card companies want us to believe that the reason credit card interest rates and fees are too high is that the silly consumer just doesn't want to shop for cheaper credit.

The truth is very, very different. Those beautifully printed solicitations for credit cards that are everywhere these days almost never give you all, or even most, of the information you need to make a rational choice of one card over another.

Annual fees, interest rates, grace periods, cash advance charges, late fees, overlimit fees, account closing fees, fees piled on fees piled on fees—all these are rarely mentioned on those beautiful applications. The credit card companies just do not want to tell the customers about prices. Indeed, only when Congressman Charles Schumer of New York introduced and passed a bill in 1988 requiring the card companies to put what's called the Schumer Box (which discloses the annual fee, interest rate, and a few other vital items) on most of the credit card companies' solicitations and applications could the consumer figure out what some of the costs of using a card would be without actually applying for it, sight unseen.

How could anyone have compared card costs when it was impossible to find out what the card costs were? The card companies liked it that way. It helped fatten company profits no end. That's why they fought so hard against Congressman Schumer's disclosure efforts.

It used to be that only *after* your application had been accepted did the card company have to tell you what it was going to charge you for the card, and then only in itsy-bitsy almost unreadable type.* After you applied for a card it was too late to compare prices. That is why the card companies liked that setup. Why compete if you don't have to?

If you, pre–Schumer Box, tried to find out what a card would cost you before you applied, you would have discovered that you probably could not, even by calling the card company. The people who answered the phone did not have the answers to questions about the cost of the company's card. Or if they did, they had been told not to answer those sorts of questions.

The Schumer Box does help. The example below shows how. It provides *some* basic information on card costs. But the information is far from complete.

You'll note that there is no mention of cash advance fees, overlimit fees, or late fees in the sample box. While the card company *may* put such fees in the Schumer Box, it doesn't have to. So many companies somehow can't find room in the box and bury those very high,

## SAMPLE SCHUMER BOX

| Annual Percentage Rate (APR) | Grace period for repayment of balances for purchases | Annual fee | Minimum finance charge | Method of computing balance for purchases |
| --- | --- | --- | --- | --- |
| 5.9% fixed introductory rate until the first day of the billing cycle that includes 7/1/2001; a 17.99% fixed rate thereafter. | You have 20 to 25 days from the date of the periodic statement (provided you paid your previous balance in full by the due date). | None | $.50 in any month that a finance charge is payable. | Two-cycle average daily balance method (including the new purchases). |

---

*California passed a law, effective in the middle of 1987, that requires *partial* up-front disclosure on credit card applications. It was a start. Unfortunately, a Consumer Action survey showed that many credit card companies were just ignoring the law. But then, as you will discover as you read along, that is standard operating procedure for many credit card companies.

extremely profitable fees in small type outside the prominent Schumer Box. No, they're not really supposed to put what those fees are in such little tiny type, but somehow it happens. And the Federal Reserve Board regulations on the Schumer Box let card companies get away with no mention at all of things such as fees for reissuing a lost or stolen card (yes, there are actually card companies that charge you for replacing a lost or stolen card—how can it be a good idea to punish the cardholder when he or she reports missing cards?), fees for providing you a copy of your statement, or application fees.

Even *with* the Schumer Box, card companies are still looking for, and finding, ways to avoid disclosing the costs of cards, even the costs that are in the box. For example, many solicitations for preapproved cards prominently tout their "low, low" introductory interest rates of, say, 5.9 percent. But many of those solicitations do not fully disclose when that introductory rate ends or what the new, higher rate will be. A low introductory come-on rate that lasts only a couple of months before going up to a super-high 19 or 21 percent annual interest rate is no bargain.

What does it cost you to have a credit card? Probably more than you think. The five main things that determine your costs are:

1. Annual fee
2. Interest charges on purchases
3. Grace period
4. Cash advance fees, late fees, overlimit fees, etc., and interest charges
5. The way the interest charges on purchases are figured

## Annual Fees

The annual fee is the first and clearest cost of having a credit card. The services offered by cards that charge the highest annual fees are mostly the same as those provided by the less costly or no-annual-fee cards. All of them let you charge your purchases at hundreds of thousands, even millions, of places around the United States and the world.

And sometimes the more expensive cards do not offer services that measure up to the cheaper ones. For example, American Express and Diners Club cards are accepted by many fewer stores and restaurants than Visa and MasterCard are. This is true both in the United States and abroad.

It stands to reason, since it costs the store less to take the bank cards than it does to take the Amex or Diners card. Thus, less pricey places can absorb the cost of the bank cards while only the more expensive places can pay what Amex and Diners charge (which they do because they think their affluent business-type customers prefer to pay with the "prestige" cards).

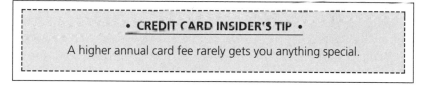

**• CREDIT CARD INSIDER'S TIP •**

A higher annual card fee rarely gets you anything special.

Another example: Diners Club charges $80 for its basic card. American Express charges around $55. Yet the Diners card is accepted in fewer places than the American Express card and it offers a range of services which is, in my estimation, less valuable for most than those offered by Amexco's card. When I asked a Diners customer service rep why its card cost more than the Amex card, she gave a terrific answer: "We do not discriminate between customers like some companies that have levels of cards [meaning American Express, with its gold and platinum cards], each with a different annual fee. All of our customers get our best service." Diners, give that woman a raise!

### Interest Rates

Many folks don't know that interest rates are different from one card issuer to the next or think the differences are not large. But they are large—in fact, *very* large at times. Some rates are relatively low, other rates are absurdly high.

That is not the only interest rate difference between card issuers. There is also a big difference in the way they figure interest rates. Some credit card companies offer rates and ways of figuring rates that are not too bad for you. Others have very clever ways of ripping off their customers.

If you know what to look for you will save yourself lots of bucks. If you don't know what to look for, your bank account will suffer. And some credit card company will be very happy.

It's no accident that credit card interest rates can be hard to understand. Interest rates can be figured in a variety of simple and not-so-simple ways. Banks have spent a long time developing the not-so-simple ways, and working to make them more and more confusing. Bankers do this to hoodwink customers, keep profits high, and keep customers confused. People who do not understand what is going on are easier to rip off.

Indeed, the banks have made computation of credit card interest so complex that even many bank employees do not understand how it's done. This is especially true of the kindly folks who attempt to answer your calls at the credit card service center. "Even bank personnel cannot explain the [interest] accounting without resorting to worksheets on which they lay out two month's worth of activity day by day," says consumer beat reporter S. J. Diamond in the *Los Angeles Times.*

The banks like it that way. They use at least six different methods of charging you interest. All credit card companies *could* use the same method of figuring interest to make it easy for you to compare costs from one card to the next. There is no reason that the Congress or the Federal Reserve Board could not take one understandable method and require all card companies to use it.

But consumer confusion means profit for the card companies. And the card companies have a lot of clout with the Fed and the Congress. The Federal Reserve Board ought to do something, but it hasn't gotten around to it yet.

And now credit card companies use computers to make figuring out interest rates even more confusing. Before computers, interest rates had to be somewhat easy to work out. Otherwise, the companies' employees could not do all the calculations needed to compute the interest on accounts. Now computers figure the interest on your account in a microsecond using methods that would take a clerk days or months to figure out with an adding machine.

The federal Truth in Lending Laws, bitterly fought by bankers, are supposed to force the banks to tell customers honestly and understandably about interest rates. Truth in Lending *is* a big improvement. But the Federal Reserve Board, which by law is responsible for guiding the banks along the right path, has yet to force full disclosure.

Political pressure from the banks is one reason, along with other factors, such as the probability that if the Fed did fight to let the average person understand interest rates, Fed staffers might not be so popular at bankers' conventions anymore. Or Fed folks might not be able to switch to good jobs at the banks when they leave the Fed. Whatever the reason, in my view, the Fed has not protected the consumer as it should have.

### Shopping for a Good Interest Rate

Given the confusion generated by the industry on interest rates, what should you do?

First, be aware that the interest rate and the way it is figured are of major importance to you. Because they determine how much interest you will pay if you don't or can't pay your bill off in full each and every month. They determine whether you will even have any interest at all to pay.

Federal law requires that each and every bill you get from a card issuer have the interest rate clearly written on the front. Two interest rates, in fact: the annual percentage rate, which is the yearly rate, and the periodic rate. The periodic rate is the monthly rate, since you usually get billed once a month. The two rates are really exactly the same rate, but figured over different time periods.

> ### • CREDIT CARD INSIDER'S TIP •
>
> When you pay off your charge account in full each month, the method of charging interest does not matter since you will not be paying any. So try hard to pay your balance in full every month. Paying off your card accounts in full every month is one of the smartest ways to manage your money.

How do you tell if the interest rate on your card is a good one? The rates as I write run from 2.9 percent (terrific!) to 25 percent or higher (horrible!) annually. These days, you are probably not going to easily find a 2.9 percent card (this sort of very low rate is generally limited to special teaser introductory direct mail offers, although many folks sign up for the teaser rate and move on to another teaser rate card when the rate goes up in six months). But by looking around, you should be able to find a card that does not demand more than 12 percent or at most 15 percent.

The difference, on an average balance of $2,000 over a year, from a, say, 10 percent okay rate to a 25 percent horrid rate is $280. This is a lot to pay a card company for doing absolutely nothing extra or special for you.

### Grace Periods

The grace period is the time after you buy something during which you can pay the bill and not have to pay any interest. Traditionally, you had twenty-five or thirty days from the day your bill was sent to you to pay it in full without any interest charges being added on to the amount due. The grace period is a tradition, not a law.

This tradition comes from the way merchants ran (and some still run) their store charge operations. Long before there were plastic credit cards, many stores let their customers put their purchases "on the account." And they allowed the customer a month or so after billing to pay up.

---

#### • CREDIT CARD INSIDER'S TIP •

Only a few credit card issuers have yet gathered enough nerve to try and charge you interest from the day you make your purchase rather than giving you twenty-five or thirty days from the billing date interest-free (although some card companies are pushing to cut back to fifteen or twenty days). You certainly do not want to be the customer of such a money-hungry credit card company. If you cannot get a reasonable, interest-free free-ride period from the credit card company you are dealing with, find another one fast!

---

When credit cards first appeared, the credit card companies followed the same policy. They had to in order to compete with the store accounts. Now that card companies dominate the financial marketplace, they would very much like to finish off the grace period, or as they call it among themselves, the free-ride period. They would like you to pay interest from the day you buy something until the day you pay it off in full.

Some banks have actually had the nerve to put this immediate interest plan into effect, often camouflaged with advertising claims of "lower interest rates" or "a lower annual fee." The disguise is needed to keep outraged customers from looking for a new card company.

Fortunately, so far, the grace period has managed to survive in the banking world. Killing off the grace period would be a very bad deal for you, the consumer. Banks started out promoting their credit cards as cost-free to you if you paid the bill within the grace period. That was to bring in the customers. Then they thought up annual fees and all kinds of other fees. Now they want to get rid of the grace period so that you will always be paying interest.

Many banks now (and merchants, too) have a policy that keeps the grace period, but eliminates it completely if you do not pay the balance due on your account in full before the end of the grace period. That is, if you do not pay off your balance in full each and every month you will pay interest on everything you buy. That includes even the things you pay off in full within the month after you get billed for them. That appears to be what happened to the writer of the following letter from Don Campbell's column "Consumer Views" in the *Los Angeles Times*:

> Question: Can you top this? We paid our July BankAmericard Visa account in full before the due date for $789.77. In reconciling our Security Pacific checking account statement that month, I noticed that the printout showed the value of the check to be $787.77, a difference of $2 from the amount of the original check, which I verified.
>
> Since the difference was only $2, I simply made a note of it and forgot it. That was a mistake.
>
> The next BankAmericard Visa statement showed a previous balance of $789.77 with a payment of $787.77. We owed them $2 from the previous month because of [the] error. BankAmericard Visa's response was to charge us $29.71 in finance charges, based on our new balance of $3,082.25.
>
> Because we always pay our credit card charges in full before the date due, I could not understand this finance charge. When I inquired at the card center, I was told that this outrageous financing method was determined by the card center's method for calculating interest.
>
> When I explained that the error was not ours, the representative immediately said the financing charge would be removed from our bill.
>
> . . . I remain appalled at these usurious practices. Even by today's freewheeling standards, a 1,500% return seems a bit much to pay.

---

### • CREDIT CARD INSIDER'S TIP •

When you cancel a card, you must *write* to the card company at the special billing error address on your statement and tell the company to cancel your account. You should keep a copy of the letter and proof it was received, either by enclosing a check with the letter with a notation in the letter that check number 000 is enclosed or by sending the letter certified mail, return receipt requested. Many folks just stick the card in a dresser drawer and stop using it. *This is very dangerous.* The account is still open until you tell the card company to cancel, and it will continue to appear on your credit reports, possibly harming your credit rating. Far more dangerous, an open but unused account is an invitation to fraudulent charges. Cancel in writing!

---

If you do not pay *all* of the *previous* month's balance on your card account, you will probably be charged interest on everything you charged in the previous month and in the current month, too. Not paying your card bill *in full* every month is a very expensive way to go. This billing method of the card companies is not a reasonable or fair policy. But almost all now do this. So you are stuck with this chopped-off grace period if you use a bank or store credit card.

Look out! Soon the credit card companies will have you paying interest on things *before* you buy them!

Travel and entertainment cards usually have the same grace period of twenty-five or thirty days, but, in theory at least, you *must* pay up within the grace period or lose your card. In fact, it is usually possible to stretch the period a bit since often the T&E companies will not charge interest or a late charge unless you run considerably over thirty days past due. But if you run over too often, they will eventually get upset, you could get charged fees, and your account could be closed.

### Cash Advances

Just what is a cash advance? The banks promote it as a trouble-free way you can get cash anywhere in the world. Normally, it is trouble-free (but not cost-free), at least in the United States.

Outside the United States it is a different story. Many card companies are desperately striving to find ways to make money off foreign charges. And they are succeeding.

Getting a cash advance is not like charging cash, as many folks think. It is like getting a loan. That is why American Express and the other travel and entertainment cards issued by companies that are not banks can't give you a cash advance.

What is the difference between charging cash and getting a loan? If you were charging cash when you got a cash advance, you would normally have a grace period of twenty-five days or so after you got your bill. Within that period you could pay off the charge without it costing you any interest.

*Interest on Cash Advances*

A cash advance works in a different way: you get no grace period. There is generally no way to avoid paying interest when you take out a cash advance. The cost of cash advances is difficult to understand.

First, the way the banks figure cash advance interest is *very* complicated. Second, once upon a time, in the early days of bank credit cards (around 1972), you could actually get a no-interest, no-fee, free-ride cash advance with some bank cards. Those cards gave you a grace period before interest was due on cash advances. This has not been true for a long time, but the memory of those happy days lingers on and confuses many folks' view of the current situation.

> Note: you can get no-interest cash with a card if it is not a credit card, but a Financial Death (debit) card. A debit card pulls the money out of your account right away, as soon as you get the cash at the bank. Since there is no loan involved, there is no interest. For reasons mentioned in Chapter 4, I strongly advise against debit cards. They are great for the banks, but not nearly so great for you.

It is also possible for a cash advance to cost you interest on all the things you charge, even if they would normally be interest free. How? Because some especially greedy banks eliminate the no-interest grace period when you have a cash advance outstanding on your account. If you have many purchases on your account this can be very costly.

So you have your not-so-trusty, bank-issued credit card in hand. You go into a bank (not the one that issued the card you are using) and say to the teller, "I'd like a hundred-dollar cash advance on this card." What happens, and what is it going to cost you?

First of all, the bank where you get the money should not (in fact, by their contract with Visa or MasterCard, is not permitted to) charge you anything for giving you the cash. If you ask for a cash advance of a hundred bucks, that is exactly what you should get. The bank that gives you the cash gets their cut from the bank that issued your card.*

The bank that issued the card, however, with a few exceptions, will not do anything for you at no charge, cash-advance-wise. It will almost certainly charge you interest at a high rate from the day the charge for the advance is sent to the bank card clearinghouse by the bank that gave you the cash.

### Killer Fees for Cash Advances

Many card-issuing banks have now worked up their nerve to charge a cash advance fee.

This is rather like your local department store charging you a "merchandise purchase fee" in addition to the price of your new socks. Ridiculous as it is, many banks do this. Some charge fees as high as 4 or even 5 percent of the amount you get in the cash advance. When added to the 18 or 20 percent interest you are also charged, this can give the bank an effective annual interest rate of 100 percent or even more! Not bad for the bank. But terrible for you.

Here is how the routine works.

Let's say your bank charges a 4 percent cash advance fee. On April 1, you get a $100 cash advance. On April 2, the $100 plus a $4 fee is billed to your account. On April 3, you pay off the cash advance. The total you will have to pay will be $100 plus $4 plus interest for one day at 18 percent, or 5¢. So what you pay is $4.05. That is the same as an effective annual interest rate of around 739 percent! Extended over a year at that rate the $100 cash advance would cost you $739 in interest. Even if you took thirty days to pay off the cash advance, the effective annual interest rate is still around 66 percent! No wonder banks like to charge cash advance fees!

Look hard for a bank that does not charge a cash advance fee. One

---

*Some states have a stamp tax, just like the one that brought on the Boston Tea Party, of, say, fifteen cents on a hundred-dollar transaction. So in those states, the bank will ask you for some fifteen pennies on the counter.

bank that has long offered some cards with no cash advance fee is USAA Federal Savings Bank of San Antonio, TX, 800-922-9092.

California and New York banks (and of course the infamous banks in Delaware and South Dakota, two states with shamefully weak consumer protection laws) seem to be among the worst offenders on cash advance fees. There are fairer banks outside these states that have no annual fee and also have no cash advance charge. Some even offer a lower-than-average interest rate.

Even if you find a bank that charges no cash advance fee, getting cash advances for anything other than emergencies (or when abroad; cash advances overseas can make sense as a way of cutting foreign exchange commissions and costs) is not a super idea because, even without the cash advance fee, you still will be charged interest on the cash advance from the day you take it out. Remember, there is no grace period on cash advances, even with a card that has a grace period on regular purchases.

Why pay very high interest charges just to get some cash in your hand? Write a check on your bank account or make a savings account withdrawal. Reserve cash advances for travel and for emergencies and save yourself money.

## How to Get Your Best Credit Card Deal

In shopping for the best deal from a bank in your area, the best you may be able to do for local pricing is call around to several banks, savings and loan associations, and credit unions. Ask them what their interest charges are. While you are on the phone be sure to also ask what their annual fees, grace periods, and charges on cash advances are.

Check the monthly charts in *Money* and *Kiplinger's Personal Finance Magazine*, both of which list low-rate *nationally* issued cards. There is no good reason to limit yourself to cards from local banks. You can also look in Chapter 15 for information on researching card costs on-line or check the Sunday business section of your local paper, many of which run a chart listing low-rate cards.

These five costs I talked about above in this chapter—annual fees, interest rates, how the rates are figured, grace periods, and cash advance charges—are the major things that determine how much each card will cost you.

Make photocopies of the chart below and use it when you make your calls to the card companies or to compare cards. Also ask each card company to send you an application, in case you decide to go with one of them.

When you are calling be sure to ask the person with whom you talk if he or she knows of any banks in the area with no annual fees or with very low interest rates. Sometimes the bank folks you talk with know the charges at banks all over town. Often they will be glad to tell you about a local competing bank that issues no-fee cards.

| Card company name and telephone | | | | |
|---|---|---|---|---|
| Annual fee | | | | |
| Annual interest rate | | | | |
| No-interest grace period | | | | |
| Cash advance fee | | | | |
| Overlimit fee | | | | |
| Late fee | | | | |
| Bounced payment check fee | | | | |

# 4

# The Financial Death Card—
# Or, How to Lose Your House
# by Using Plastic

## I Got a Little Upset

This chapter is dedicated to Thomas J. Morton of St. Petersburg, Florida, who in August 1983 put six rounds of .32-caliber ammunition into an automatic teller machine after it ate his cash card and refused to give him any cash. "It was the second time it happened to me," he said. "I got a little upset."

Those popular automatic teller machine (ATM), electronic funds transfer (EFT), check cards, or debit cards (all four are basically the same kind of plastic) are not credit cards at all. But they sure *look* like credit cards. Some might say that's the whole idea. These cards are very often sold in such a way as to confuse the issue and lead consumers to believe that they are getting a real credit card, with all the consumer protections a real card has and a Financial Death/debit card does not. Instead of giving you a line of credit you can use, the Financial Death Card—or debit card or check card as the card companies often call it—sucks money directly from your bank account every time you use it. No waiting—the money is removed immediately.

## The Different Kinds of Death Cards

You probably have a Death Card in your wallet right now. An automatic teller card (ATM) that you use to get cash from a bank's cash machine or from a cash machine at the supermarket is one kind of Financial Death Card.

Another kind looks like a Visa or MasterCard credit card. But it is definitely not a credit card. You can tell the difference between a bank-type credit card and a bank-type debit card only by what the card does to your finances. Let's call this kind of card the No Credit Card variety of the Financial Death Card.

The No Credit Card (or NCC) has two fishy sub-species, on-line and off-line, which can hook you and the merchants in some very tricky ways. The differences between on-line and off-line NCCs illuminate some important but little-known information about card company finances. The on-line card instantaneously pulls money out of your account, mostly by using a dial-up line that goes to the card company's computer where your account is kept. The off-line card pulls it out a day or so later, without telling the card company's computer at the time the purchase is made. The card companies charge the merchants around 2 percent of the purchase amount when you use an off-line card. And just a few cents (typically between 2.5¢ and 11¢ for each transaction, regardless of the amount of purchase) when you use an on-line card.

Not surprisingly, the banks are pushing the off-line cards, which are incredibly more profitable for them. And not surprisingly, the merchants are squawking about it. They can't see what the card companies are providing for the $10 commission paid on a $500 off-line Death Card sale beyond what they provide for the 10¢ paid on that same $500 sale when paid with an on-line card. I can't see it either. In fact some merchants, including Wal-Mart, Sears, and The Limited, are so upset by the discrepancy that they have sued Visa and MasterCard.

Both the on-line and off-line versions of Death Cards are varieties of the electronic funds transfer card, a fancy name for *trouble*. Some tricky card companies have decided to disguise the Financial Death Card by calling it an "electronic check."

If you have a cash management type of account with a stockbroker, the plastic card you use to get cash out of that account is almost certainly a Financial Death/debit card. And your entire financial future is at risk. A Death/debit card linked to a broker's cash management account gives a crook the ability to steal *all* your money, stocks, and bonds because the Death Card does not protect its holders with the

$50 maximum liability for fraudulent use that a real credit card provides. If you have a Death Card hooked to your account at your broker, your financial future is in big danger.

Some brokers have voluntarily adopted a $50 limit for customer losses on a cash management type account. If your broker is not such a one, you should switch brokers *now*. Or if you love your account representative, immediately close the cash management account, get rid of the Death Card, and keep the account rep. Do not accept your account representative's oral reassurances that you are protected for amounts over $50. Be sure you have it in writing (it should be in the account agreement papers somewhere) unless you choose to put at risk your entire financial future.

There is some movement for greater protection for debit card users. In the summer of 1997, apparently under pressure from bills introduced in Congress by Representatives Joe Kennedy and Charles Schumer, MasterCard and then Visa announced that they would change their policy and require that users of debit cards with the MasterCard or Visa logos no longer be held liable for more than $50 when there has been fraudulent use of the card.

Note that this plan is a change of MasterCard and Visa policy, not a change in the law. Policy can be changed back when the heat is off. TransUnion, Equifax, and Experian (formerly TRW), the big three credit reporting agencies, a few years ago were threatened by legislation that would have required them to provide free copies to each consumer of his or her credit report. They "voluntarily" started to provide free reports once a year, on request. The threat of legislation disappeared. So did the free credit reports. The $50 limit could similarly disappear.

Also, something like MasterCard policy is easily ignored by MasterCard-issuing banks when the only person who might try to enforce the policy is an individual consumer. A year or so from now, after having $10,000 fraudulently taken from his or her account, a consumer is not likely to know about this policy, and neither is the lawyer the consumer might consult. Laws, however, are on the books and can easily be looked up. Where do you go to look up MasterCard policy? Laws are also much harder to ignore than policy because you can go to court to enforce laws.

What's needed is a change in the law to so that consumers are properly protected.

After the Bank of America followed MasterCard's lead and announced that it too would voluntarily extend some of the protections credit card users have to debit card users, The *Los Angeles Times* editorialized: "Banks save money on debit cards because they don't have to process paper checks. In return, all users of these cards deserve at least the legal protections and disclosures of credit cards." Jon Golinger of the California Public Interest Research Group commented on the Bank of America's debit card policy change: "Its a good step to protect consumers from risks they weren't told about when they got it."

You can have a Financial Death Card/debit card that looks like a credit card, but which acts both as a Visa or MasterCard debit card *and* as an automatic teller card at the same time. A Visa/MasterCard type Death Card can be used anywhere in the world that a regular Visa or MasterCard can be used. You can pay for things with it in Kenosha or in Italy. As with the credit cards, each issuing bank sets its own terms and rules for use of the Death Card within the limits set by the law and the secret Visa or MasterCard regulations that only card companies get copies of.

## ATM Cards

All ATM cards are not alike. The automatic teller machine card given out by the local bank may be usable at just one bank or at many banks; at a few stores or at many stores. It may be usable all day and all night or only during business hours. It may be usable just in the local area or all over the country or soon, perhaps, the world. It all depends on the deals the local bank has worked out with other banks and the stores.

Banks have made big promises for ATMs and have not always delivered: thus, one midwestern bank announced that its "24 Hour Banker Machines" would be available for less than eight hours a day!

Originally ATM cards could be used just to get cash from the machines of the issuing bank. Now they are becoming much more commonly accepted and may someday be as widely taken as the Visa/MasterCard Financial Death Cards.

Recently, some banks have gotten very excited about charging fees for getting your money out of your account at their ATMs, particularly if your account is at another bank. This is very helpful for bank profits, although not so helpful for your pocketbook. Although some bankers claim that these new, heavy charges are justified by the costs of maintaining the ATM machines, this is a most dubious claim.

David W. Porges, vice president of public affairs of Coast Federal Bank, wrote to the *Los Angeles Times*: "To pay upward of $4 for a $20 withdrawal is absurd and can amount to hundreds of dollars a year. Furthermore, maintenance costs alone do not justify ATM surcharges. The older fee structure more than covered annual expenses." Mr. Porges goes on to comment on the big California banks that have imposed hefty surcharges on withdrawals from other banks *except* at the ATMs in and around the state capitol in Sacramento: "As for banks that remove surcharges on ATMs located near state capitol buildings, their intention is clear [to curry favor with or avoid angering legislators]."

Many in the banking business think that the new ATM surcharges are an attempt by the biggest banks to hurt their smaller competitors by making it very costly for small banks' customers to make ATM withdrawals from the biggest banks' machines. Since the big banks already get paid for each withdrawal by the small banks' customers, it is darn close to impossible to see any good reason for the surcharges.

The spread of the Death Card is bad news for you, especially if you don't like paying huge fees to get at your money or have an account at one of those friendly little banks the big guys want to zap.

## What You Lose with the Financial Death Card

*Float.* When you use a Death Card, your float disappears. Float is the interest you could make on money that stays in your bank account until you have to pay a bill. This is one reason card companies love the Financial Death Card: you are losing the float; they are gaining it. Real credit cards give you at least a month of float free.

*Legal Protections.* Financial Death Card users do not have the stop-payment rights users of real credit cards have. Using a Death Card is *worse* than paying by check. At least when you pay by check there is a short interval when you can stop the check. With a Death Card, the money is gone from your checking account in nanoseconds.

Thus, Death Card users lose their right to stop payment on bad merchandise or services. When you use a real credit card, you have the legal right to stop payment for sixty or more days. Further, you have much more legal protection against fraudulent use of your credit card than against fraudulent use of your Death Card.

*Improved Credit Rating.* Having and using a Financial Death/debit card will not improve your credit report, since no credit is involved when you use the card. It is simply a way of removing money you already have out of your bank account to buy something. When you buy something with a real credit card the company lends you the money with which to buy the goods.

Credit reports are information collected from your creditors about your payment history on recent card accounts, car loans, and so forth which credit bureaus, including TransUnion, Equifax, and Experian (formerly TRW), sell to potential creditors so they can use the information to decide if they want to give you credit.

Since no credit is given with a Financial Death Card, using it cannot have any effect on your credit report. If you have no credit record it will not help you get one. If you have a bad credit record it will not help you improve it.

*All the Money in Your Bank Account.* If your Financial Death Card is stolen or lost, the thief can take all the money you have in the bank. Unless you act right away, there may be no way of getting it back from the bank, even if the bank knew that a thief and not you was getting money.

*All Your Money in the World.* With a Financial Death Card, a crook can take all the money in your bank accounts and then get into your overdraft and other line-of-credit accounts. The thief can use his access to those accounts to drive you thousands and thousands of dollars in debt. Again, some protections do exist, but the burden is on you to act quickly.

*Real Personal Identification.* The "security" code used with the Financial Death Card is exceedingly insecure. The personal identification number, or PIN, as the credit card companies call it, does not give you security and does not identify you.

The number is easy for a dishonest credit card company employee to come by. Crooks outside the credit card company can also get the number by using inside contacts or by computer hacking.

The PIN number does not have the outstanding security feature of the time-honored identification feature used on checks and credit card slips: your signature. You can look at a signature and almost always say, "This is my John Hancock" or "This is a forgery." No one can tell by looking at a PIN punched into a computer terminal whether you or a crook punched in the number.

Indeed, card companies now are eager to hand out Death Cards that can be used without even the small security a PIN provides. Anyone can use such a card when it is lost or stolen; and you, the completely innocent cardholder, may well get stuck with the bill.

## Death Card Horror Stories

COUNTERFEITER'S EQUIPMENT IS READILY AVAILABLE
Moreover, all the necessary equipment needed to produce perfect cards is widely available, including laser coder scanners (which can transfer the information of one magnetic strip onto another), corner rounders (which allow for the proper card shaping) and card embossing hardware.

—*Card News*

*The All-Too-Real Nightmare of Lawrence and Georgene Kruser*
Consider the unfortunate tale of the Kruser family of California, as recounted in the case of *Kruser v. Bank of America* (230 Cal.App.3d 741, 1991).

Mr. and Mrs. Kruser each had a Versatel card and personal identification numbers for automatic teller access to their joint checking account. Some unknown crook made forty-seven ATM withdrawals from their account, totaling $9,020. The Krusers told the Bank of America about the fraudulent charges within a few days of getting the statements showing them.

The bank refused to credit the Krusers' account for the fraudulent charges and the Krusers sued. The appellate court, interpreting the consumer-unfriendly federal Electronic Funds Transfer Act, decided that the Krusers were on the hook (and the Bank of America was off the hook) for the $9,020. Reason: The Krusers believed that Mr. Kruser's Versatel card had been destroyed. A few months later, the bank sent them a statement showing a $20 unauthorized withdrawal apparently using that card, but because Mrs. Kruser (who reviewed the statements for the couple) was in the hospital for major surgery then and was recuperating at home for many months more, the $20 fraud went undiscovered for months. Seven or eight months later, the forty-seven fraudulent withdrawals were made, the initial $20 fraudulent charge was identified, and the bank was notified of all the fraud; the bank refused to credit the Krusers' account.

The court decided that, under the federal Electronic Funds Transfer Act, if there is ever a fraudulent charge on your Financial Death Card, and if you don't notify the bank of the first fraud within sixty days, you will have to pay for *all* fraudulent charges made later on the account.

The judges seemed to think this was a good thing, that it would somehow make consumers more alert and likely to report fraudulent charges. The judges thought that the Krusers should be on the hook because there was a chance that the bank could have taken steps to keep the later forty-seven thefts from happening if it had been told about the initial $20 theft. The judges didn't explain why the Krusers should pay for the incredible lack of security in the Death Card system rather than the bank, which set the whole system up. And they didn't explain why if exactly the same thing had happened with one of the Krusers' credit cards, they would have been legally liable for no more than $50 total.

The Bank of America has certainly had some serious problems with automatic teller fraud. Denise Gellene of the *Los Angeles Times* reports that an ATM fraud ring took at least $100,000 from BoA customers' accounts. The Secret Service says that the thieves would park vans outside BoA branches, secretly videotape ATM transactions, and collect discarded receipts to get the information they needed to counterfeit ATM cards. The videotaping, with a high-powered camera, let the crooks see the identification number customers punched into the machine. BoA customers were especially vulnerable because the BoA ATM machines printed the entire card number on receipts. "The card number, encoded on the magnetic strip on the back of the ATM card, is one of two numbers needed to tap an account."

Bank of America announced that it would stop printing the entire number on the ATM receipts. Secret Service Agent Greg James argues the change was a direct result of the fraud. The bank said the change was coincidental and that it has not alerted customers about the fraud because doing so "would cause undue concern."

The real message of the Kruser case is that the government has not provided proper protection for debit card users. Perhaps this sort of legal protection wasn't important many years ago when the law that is currently in effect was made and use of debit cards was relatively uncommon, but today the law should be changed and you should know how to protect yourself as best you can against the horrendous losses possible under the present regime.

You can take certain protective measures to limit potential loss. For example, have your Death Card account at a bank where you do no other business and keep a minimal amount of money in the account, thus limiting your potential loss to fraud. A bank or credit union which offers a checking account with a small minimum balance and no monthly fee would be a good bet. Often such account offers are advertised in the Sunday business section of big-city newspapers.

Otherwise, you might end up being surprised when your bank starts to foreclose on your house. Me, I wonder why the Bank of America took such a hard line against its customers, the Krusers. I'm sure glad I don't have a BoA Versatel card.

### Loss of Valuable Legal Rights

When you use a debit card you *lose* the legal protections you have when you use a real credit card. The card companies would like you to think that there is no problem here. Errors and fraud are easily fixed, they claim. And perhaps they would be, at least sometimes, if card companies would follow the law.

Can you stop payment on a Financial Death/debit card? No way! When you use a Financial Death Card to make a payment, under federal law, it is just as though you had paid cash. It is even worse for you than if you had paid by check, because there is no check to stop and there is no check processing time. The taking of money out of your account is instantaneous. You do not have the right real credit card users have to refuse to pay for unsatisfactory merchandise after the purchase is made.

There is one minor exception to no stop payment with a Death Card. Suppose you have arranged in advance for payments to be made regularly from your account (say, to cover your monthly apartment rent). Then you can stop the previously authorized payment by telling the bank three or more business days before the payment is scheduled to be made.

If this doesn't seem like much of a stop-payment right, that's because it isn't. In fact, it's *worse* than paying cash. At least if you pay cash, you can decide not to buy right up to the time of purchase. With a preauthorized Death Card payment you have to decide not to buy *three days* before the payment is made. Such a deal!

## Advantages of Financial Death Cards

You may have noticed that I am not a big fan of Financial Death/debit cards. But there are a few very modest advantages.

One is getting cash. With the Visa/MasterCard variety Death Card you can get cash almost anywhere in the world without paying interest charges as you would have to do with a cash advance on a real credit card. This is only fair, since the money you are getting is yours— money that is already in your account.

Second, with an ATM type Death Card you can get cash (if the machine is working) any time of the day or night without waiting in line for a teller—if there is no line at the machine.

Problems exist even with the advantages. The card companies, in an amazing display of gall, have implemented plans to charge you a fee when you use the Death Card to get at your very own money. This charge, of course, destroys the one Death Card advantage of world-wide, no-cost access to your bank account. A vast consumer protest in 1996 when the card companies changed the rules to allow just about any cash terminal operator to charge just about any fee he or she desires to users of that terminal may yet lead to legal elimination of all such fees. That would be a good thing. Also, some ATM networks are now sticking cardholders with an extra fee for using a Death Card overseas. Check with the bank that issued your Death Card before you travel and get a written statement of possible overseas charges.

First, banks closed lots of branches, fired lots of tellers, made it harder and harder to visit or get your money. And they pushed customers to use ATMs and Death Cards to get their money, touting the money-saving efficiencies of electronic transactions. Now, having forced their customers into Death Card mode, banks want to charge big bucks for the almost-mandatory use of Death Cards. The only practical alternative appears to be using a credit card to obtain cash advances, something you have to generally go to the bank to do.

The "advantages" of the Death Card certainly do not outweigh the terrible financial dangers that await you if you use the Financial Death Card.

## Stolen or Lost Death Cards

Federal law regulates what you can be held liable for if your Death Card is lost or stolen. Unfortunately, it doesn't provide much protection.

### *Your Loss Limited to, at Most, $50*

You are not liable for more than $50 *if* you notify the card issuer within two business days of learning that your card is lost or stolen. Note that this does not mean within two days of the loss or theft, but within two days after you find out about the theft or loss. Suppose your card is lost on May 10, but you don't notice it's gone until May 20; you have two days from May 20 to give the issuer notice and so limit your liability to $50. The notice does not have to be in writing, but it sure would be smart to call and follow up with a hand-delivered notice or certified letter, return receipt requested (keep a copy for your records).

*Example.* Grendel stole the Maid of Bath's ATM card and her access code. The next day Grendel took out $400, everything the Maid had in her bank account. Two weeks later he took out another $900, which was paid out of the Maid's overdraft line of credit.

The Maid didn't know her card and code had been stolen until she got a statement from the Bank of the Thames. She called the bank immediately and reported the fraudulent transactions (carefully writing down the date, time, and person spoken to for her records). The Maid is liable for, at most, $50, even though Grendel got $1,300 from the Bank of the Thames.

### *Your Loss Limited to, at Most, $500*

You are not liable for more than $500 *if* you notify the card issuer within sixty days after a statement showing an unauthorized transaction is *mailed* to you. Note that doesn't mean the day you get the statement, but the day it is put in the mail to you, so you really have less than sixty days to give notice to limit your loss to $500.

*Example.* The Maid of Bath neglects to look at her statement showing the first two fraudulent withdrawals by Grendel until sixty-one days after it was mailed to her. Then eighty days after the statement was mailed Grendel strikes again, withdrawing another $2,000 and hitting the ceiling on the Maid's credit line. The bank immediately calls the Maid, and she tells it the charges are fraudulent. The Maid would be liable for $1,350 ($1,300 for fraudulent withdrawals more than sixty days after statement mailed, $50 for fraudulent withdrawals within the sixty day period).

---

**• CREDIT CARD INSIDER'S TIP •**

If you decide that you simply *must* have a Financial Death Card, you can limit your possible losses:

1. Have your debit/Financial Death Card account at a bank where you have no other accounts or loans at all (be sure to look for a no-fee account).

2. Do not keep more than a few hundred dollars (at most) in the account. This strategy keeps the amount you can lose to the Death Card relatively low.

3. Call to report theft or loss of the card *immediately. Follow up with a written notice by certified mail or one personally delivered by you to the bank* and keep notes on your call and a copy of the written notice (the bank can request a follow-up written notice within ten days of your phone call).

4. If you have a PIN ID number to use with the Death Card, don't write it on or keep it with your card. And don't let people see you punch in the number when you're using a terminal.

5. Always get a receipt from the ATM and *never* leave your receipt behind. Take it home and shred it or flush it after using it to check your statement.

---

Once you give the bank notice, it has forty-five days (no more) to investigate and resolve the matter. Let's hope your bank's investigation and resolution consists of more than just saying, "Pay up, you attempted rip-off artist," due to a lack of desire on the part of the bank to eat the fraud losses if it can finagle you into paying charges you don't legally owe.

### The Financial Death Card Takes a Holiday

M.R., a Death Card holder in San Antonio, wrote to *Consumer Reports Travel Letter* about his overseas adventures with his card.

> [In France] I had to try at least five banks to find a machine that worked with my card. Others said, "Your bank denied the transaction" or "the transaction could not be completed."
>
> To make matters worse, two of those denied transactions, where I got no cash, appeared on my statement as withdrawals when I returned home. Luckily, I had kept all my receipts, and my bank was able to correct the problem.

In other words, the international (and domestic) ATM system is far from perfect and you may easily be the victim of its failings. You may have a problem getting cash from an ATM and find that the overseas bank claims you got the cash and must pay up, putting the transaction on your statement and leaving you to do battle with the bank that issued your Death Card. I think M.R. was very lucky that his bank resolved the problem for him. What if the bank had told him to go back to France and prove that he didn't get the cash, as could very well happen?

So, I'm still waiting for someone to explain to me why I should want to have a Death Card. The card companies love 'em. As far as I am concerned, they are way too dangerous. Maybe you should think about whether you really need one too. If you decide that you must have one (and they are convenient) use the information in this chapter to do what you can to cut the risk.

# 5

# The Credit Card That Can Eat Your House

Would you like to go on a credit card spending spree? And perhaps pay for it by losing your home? The credit card companies seem to think that you would.

The credit card companies want it called a home equity loan [HEL] or a preapproved home equity overdraft credit line of protection or a home equity access credit line. I call it a second mortgage.

Fancy names or plain, they all mean the same thing: financial poison. You bet your home against your ability to pay back credit card bills.

This is not a good bet. Only someone whose family had its home foreclosed away from it by a bank can know how evil a thing the second mortgage can be.

The card companies have a new twist with their "home equity access credit line" second mortgages. Some like to pass the money out through a plastic card that *looks* like a credit card, but which is really a Financial Death/debit card. The companies think that plastic card makes the second mortgage seem less mortgage-like (which it does). And it also takes important legal protections away from you, when the card companies make that plastic card a Financial Death/debit card. See Chapter 4 for some pretty scary stuff you need to know before you start running one through automatic teller machines.

Some home equity loan/second mortgage deals are hooked into Death/debit cards; others into what at first glance appear to be real credit cards. Either kind of second-mortgage plastic is a bad deal. Still others use what look like cash-advance checks in combination with pseudo-credit cards.

The HEL shuffle works like this. The card company gives you a credit card with an incredibly high credit limit (just about what it thinks it could sell your house for at a foreclosure auction) and with perhaps relatively low interest rates. That is the bait. If you have problems paying the company back, it takes your house and sells it out from under you. That is the big, sharp, deadly hook.

The card companies like this scheme so much that they got Congress to provide a special tax deal for the interest you pay on this second mortgage. Interest you pay on most other kinds of credit is no longer deductible from your income for federal tax purposes. But interest on second mortgage credit cards is (with limitations) deductible.

This is a sweet deal—for the card companies and second mortgagers. Somehow they often neglect to tell you that, in many cases, second mortgage interest may not be lawfully deductible, especially if the amount of the HEL line of credit is greater than the amount you paid for your house years ago, or if it's not what's called a "purchase money" mortgage.

It's a sweet deal for the HEL pushers, but not for you. Tax-deductible interest on a credit card payment is not worth a gamble with your family's home, especially when it may not really be deductible after all. This is not what the card companies will tell you. "Greatest thing since snake oil!" they claim. We've all seen plenty of ads pushing HELs for things like buying a boat, taking a trip to Europe, even buying expensive jewelry.

For the card companies it is a win-win situation. If you manage to pay them back they get big up-front fees, hefty interest rates on what you borrow, and big profits. If you do not pay them back, they get your house. For cheap.

> "Morally, I and my management here feel [the home equity line of credit] was not designed to be used for such things as day-to-day credit card purchases," says one ethical banker, Joseph L. Grabowski of Carteret Savings Bank of New Jersey. "It is not a good idea to mix these."

Grabowski, quoted in *Investors Daily,* also said that he is concerned with the possible increased credit card fraud tied to such big lines of credit. "Equity lines of credit," says John Pollick, publisher of the *Bank Credit Card Observer*, also in *Investors Daily*, "could lead people into extraordinary debt."

## Real Credit Cards Are Unsecured

The card the company may hand out with a home equity loan *looks* like a real credit card. But looks can be deceiving. It is most likely not a real credit card, but a pseudo-credit card, a clever kind of fake.

The key difference is that a real credit card gives you unsecured credit. This means that if you have a dispute with the card company or if you cannot pay off what you charge, the company has no legal right to go after your money or property until it has won a court case against you.

That is not so easy for the card company to do. It is very expensive and can easily take years if you fight back a little. The companies do not like to do this, especially for the $2,000 or $3,000 usually involved in ordinary credit card problems. Most companies do not think they can make money by going to court over such matters.

And when you use a real credit card you have all the legal protections I talk about throughout this book.

## Fake Credit Cards Are Secured

"Secured" sounds like a good thing. But if you are a credit card user it is definitely *not* a good thing, especially when the security is your family's house. If you have a dispute with the card company or have problems paying the loan, the card company can (and likely will) grab your house out from under you. And you may not have the legal protections that real credit card users do have.

This is why card companies are in love with pseudo-credit cards and "home equity loans." The pseudo-credit card is what the boys in the card industry call an access device. It lets you get at money, but it does not, by itself, give you any credit at all. You can use this access device only to get at money you have already been lent on a secured basis. The access device looks like a real Visa or MasterCard credit card, but it is not a credit card at all. In fact, it is a species of the dread Financial Death Card.

This all may seem a bit confusing. The credit card companies may have designed it that way.

Just recently, I've been hearing tons of ads on news radio stations for HELs that claim to lend you 125 percent or more of the value of the equity in your house. That sounds great until you figure out that the interest rate is around 20 percent and the up-front fees and points are 25 percent or more, meaning you certainly get no more than the value of the equity you have in the house, and that you are putting your family's home at risk.

Here are some other problems with home equity loans/second mortgages:

1. Balloon payments, where after ten or so years you have to come up with the big remaining balance of the loan. The monthly payments are not enough to pay off the loan, even if you make every single one on time—so that at the end of the loan term, you must come up with big bucks to keep your house.

2. Variable interest rates with no limit as to how high the rates can go. Many HELs have no interest rate cap. Such a cap would obviously protect you—against the lender.

   Remember years ago when mortgage interest rates were around 20 percent? How would you like to see the monthly payment on your second mortgage go from $900 to $2,700 or more? It could happen, with no limit on how high the floating interest rate can go.

3. Points are charged on the entire amount of the line of credit granted, even if you borrow only a small fraction of that line of credit (each point is a 1 percent fee on the entire amount to be lent, charged up-front by the lender). Suppose your credit line is $100,000 and the lender demands a rather steep four points, or 4 percent of that as a fee. And suppose you end up borrowing only $10,000. You could pay $4,000 in points, or 40%! So you would be paying back $14,000 plus interest.

Some credit card companies also use "home equity loan checks" in their second-mortgage schemes. You may have gotten junk mail with a "Write Yourself a Check for One Hundred Thousand Dollars!" pitch. The access device is a check, but the scheme is the same. The scheme is "You bet your house."

This cannot be stressed enough: the home equity loan/second mortgage scheme is too full of pitfalls for anyone to mess around with.

# Credit Card Record-Keeping

Should you hang on to your credit card records? Absolutely! Some folks toss theirs as soon as they pay 'em.

This is definitely *not* recommended.

## Why Keep Records?

You should keep your records for at least six years. Your account bills are valuable tax records. The Internal Revenue Service can go back as far as six years, sometimes even further, in auditing your tax records. Just as important, you need them if you have to do battle with a card issuer or a merchant to protect your rights.

The disclosure statement that you *must* by law get when your card comes in the mail is also *very important*. It is the contract between you and the card company. You may need it later, so *save* it along with your card bills. I suggest that you staple it to the bill it comes with and the envelope it came in and then put it in your file folder for that credit card account.

One aggressive attorney suggests that consumers keep a big barrel right by the front door. Then they should toss in the barrel every receipt and bill they get. Next, keep the barrel forever.

That may be going too far, but the idea is sound. Hang on to your records. Someday you may wish you had them.

## What to Keep

Save the disclosure statement/credit card agreement that must come with your new card. A new statement must be sent to you on already-open accounts at least once a year. Be sure to write the date it came on it, and save any changes in the terms of the contract sent you later in the same way. Card companies like to shift the terms of their deal with you by sending out new contracts, and you or your lawyer may need all the different copies to solve a problem. Most disclosure statements are almost incomprehensible without serious study, but hang on to 'em anyhow. Keep in mind that often the card companies like to send out important changes in terms (like doubling the interest rate on your account or raising the overlimit fee to $25) on little tiny slips of paper stuck in with the monthly statement. They never put important changes on a phosphorescent orange, full-size page with a headline reading: "Important Changes!" Maybe they would prefer that you don't find out about such changes until you get stuck? Save all the notices, no matter how obscure looking, that come in on your account.

Once a month the card company sends you a printed summary of the transactions on your account. Neither bank card nor store card companies send you a copy of the transaction slip that you signed at the merchant. You can make them send you photocopies of the slips if you need to (see page 69).

Should you save the copy you get from the merchant when you buy something? Well, you *should*. But to tell the truth, plenty of folks don't always do it. Somehow, the slips end up crumpled and illegible in the bottom of your pocket or wrinkled and torn in your wallet. Or turn into a mass of yellowish pulp in the bottom of the washing machine.

What you *should* do is save all the little slips and compare them with your monthly statement. That is what the card companies will tell you to do, and it is a good idea.

For security and for tax purposes you should save the statements, but after comparing the charge slips to the charges on the statements and verifying that the charges are correct, you can get rid of the slips. I like to flush them down the toilet after ripping them into pieces, but then I've handled credit card fraud cases that made me *very* aware of just how dangerous it can be to put your charge slips, or anything with your name and card number on it, in the garbage. Dumpster divers, folks who troll through trash looking for information to be used in card fraud, can show up anywhere.

Cards such as American Express, which claim higher status, used to send you a copy of the transaction slips along with the printed summary. Now they just send a mini photocopy. American Express and the other companies call it "country club" billing, since sending a copy of the charge slip was the way snooty clubs used to bill their members. It is a better system since you have a chance to look at the charge slips and see if that is really your signature on the bottom. This system is also more expensive for the company. It costs more to handle paper than to deal with electronic impulses.

If you have a card that uses country club billing, save both the summary pages and the mini transaction slips.

Check the bill over *carefully* when it comes. Bills are *often* wrong. And you have less than sixty days from the day the bill comes to use most of your billing error correction rights. If the statement is okay, put the slips and summary pages back into the envelope. Some folks like to unfold everything and staple it together with the envelope at the back.

Finally, put the envelope in a pack with the others for the current year. Use a rubber band to hold each year's together. Then stick the packet in a drawer or box with earlier years so you can find them when you need them.

Keep the envelopes the bills are mailed in because they usually have a postmark on them that shows when and where they were mailed and because this will help you pick out a specific month's statement when you want to refer to it. When you first receive the bill, write something like "rec'd 12/25/2003" and your initials on the envelope and staple it behind the statement.

## Keep a Log of Phone Conversations

Any time you have a phone conversation with a card company worker, be sure to note it in your log, kept in the file for that credit card account. The log note should include the date; who you talked with, including his or her title and phone number; and what was said. If you do not keep such notes, you will never remember who said what to whom when. Computer users may want to do this on a personal information manager program such as Desk Top Organizer on their home computer. Such a program can automatically enter the date and time of each entry and keep all the notes organized, but you can certainly do the same thing with a notebook and a pencil.

It is amazing how different your idea of what was discussed and the card company's idea can be. And how nice and useful it can be to tell Mr. Banks: "Contrary to what you say, Mr. Banks, my records show that you *did* promise in our phone conversation of January ninth to correct the overcharge on my bill from Ignoble Department Stores."

An example of a phone log entry is below. The notation *tt* means telephone call to and *tf* means telephone call from.

| 12/20/2003 2:22 P.M. | tt 22nd Savings bank customer service at 800-666-6666 | Spoke to Mr. Banks. He told me that it was impossible to stop payment on the repairs not done on my car and that I was a bad person for even asking about such a thing. I told him to note in the file on my account that I had requested a stop payment on the $900 charge from SicTrans. |
|---|---|---|
| 1/3/2004 | tf 22nd S.B. customer service | Call from Ms. Banker. She says they have my certified billing error letter of 12/21/2003 and will be charging back to SicTrans the $900. She will send me confirming letter today, at my request. Her direct number is 800-666-6666, ext. 666. |

## Getting Copies of Your Charge Slips

The law requires the card companies to send you copies of your slips if you ask for them within sixty days of the day the company mailed you the bill that shows the charge you want a slip for.

Can the company charge you for the copies? No, not legally, if when you ask for the slips, you say you suspect a billing error. But that doesn't mean the card company won't try. One card company scam is to try and charge you for copies of your slips when you ask for them to investigate a billing error. The company *says* it will refund the charge *if* it decides there is a billing error. Otherwise, says the company, you have to pay from $3 to $5 for a photocopy of a slip the law says you should get for free! Why do some companies do this? Obviously to discourage folks from demanding investigations into billing errors. I expect a lawsuit concerning this little evasive tactic one of these days. It is, after all, illegal under the federal Truth in Lending Act for the card companies to try and discourage or "chill" cardholders from exercising their rights. If a card company tries this routine on you, you may want to write and tell them that it's illegal and you want copies at no charge.

Theoretically, you may be charged if you ask for the slips for tax record purposes. This was one exception apparently considered when the Truth in Lending Act was passed. But, since the act was passed, the IRS has changed the rules on what you need to prove deductions and now accepts your monthly statement alone as proof of most deductions. So it's very unlikely this exception will come into play today.

Attempting to charge for copies in a billing error situation indicates, at best, a bad attitude on the company's part. If the card company wants you to pay five bucks for the copy of a slip, you should start thinking about changing companies. And you might want to drop a note of complaint to the credit card cops with a copy to the president of the card company.

---

**• CREDIT CARD INSIDER'S TIP •**

When asking a card company for copies of slips, say that the copies are needed "for investigation of a billing error." This will help avoid any charges for the copies.

---

Charges for copies of slips *must* be explicitly revealed in the initial disclosure statement that you get when your card comes in the mail. If the company "forgot" to tell you about them in the disclosure statement, the charge is clearly illegal.

If you ask for slips from a bank card issuer more than sixty days after the statement showing the questioned bill for the first time, you may not get them. The bank may claim that it cannot get the copies after the sixty days are up because the time for getting copies has run out. Or it may say that all it gets is electronic information on the sale from the bank that processes the merchant's credit card slips and that the merchant's bank will not send the slips after the sixty days are up.

This is not so. The slips can almost always be gotten, even years after the charge was made, especially now that most of the companies have taken to storing electronic images of charge slips on their computers. It could take quite a while, though—possibly months. Indeed, some card company operating regulations require slip copies to be available for at least a year.

You might wonder why you should pay for charges the card company is unable to show you made by producing a copy of the signed slip. Often, when the card company can't (or won't) provide a copy of the slip, the charge is fraudulent.

The law does not *make* the card company get the slips for you after sixty days, so the company may not do so unless you push. And push hard. It may help to mention to the card company that the Visa and MasterCard operating regulations require the card company to provide slips for well over sixty days after the charge. It's also good to complain to whichever of the two associations is appropriate if the card you're having a problem with is a Visa or MasterCard (association addresses are in the Resources section).

T&E and store card companies are usually more cooperative in providing copies of slips. They do it with less hassle and are usually willing to do it long after bank card companies might refuse you a copy. It is a little easier for them to get copies because the records are all in-house, under the company's control.

## Save the Envelopes?

The bill from the card company may not sport a dated postmark. It may have only the printed message "First Class Postage Paid" with no stamp or date.

Credit card companies like to send out envelopes without postmark dates on them for two reasons. One, it is, they claim, cheaper for them. Two (this they are not so eager to claim), without a dated postmark nobody can tell when the bill was really mailed. And some card companies are not above dating a bill "July 1, pay before July 25" and mailing it July 15. This cuts into the time you have to pay the bill and makes it much more likely that you will end up paying interest on your charge purchases.

Write something like "rec'd July 18" with your initials on the bills as they come in. That way you will have a record of the delivery date, even if there is no postmark to give the date of mailing.

Keep in mind that the date on a postage meter postmark is not proof of the day a letter was mailed. It is easy (although illegal) for a mailer to put the wrong date on an envelope. I got a bill which arrived at 8:55 A.M. on May 1. The meter mark stated it was mailed two thousand miles away the same day. Doubtful. And I love the letters from card companies dated August 15 which say something like: "We must have your response to this letter by August 25 or the questioned charge will be recharged to your account." But the letter shows clearly that it was postmarked August 27, and it was received on August 30.

## Keep Those Letters!

Besides keeping your credit card bills you should also keep any letters the company sends you. These include notices such as "over credit limit $1.12; please remit $21.12 immediately," as well as replies to any letters you might send to the company.

You must keep copies of any letters you send to the company. And you should not try to resolve any serious problems with the company without sending them a letter.

It is okay to call the credit card company for information. But for any billing or other problem be *sure* to write. There are two reasons for this:

1. The only sure way to protect your legal rights is to write a letter. A phone call will not do it, nor will ten phone calls.
2. If you have a problem with the company or with a merchant you will have done what lawyers call building a record.

## Love and Paper

If you get into a serious fight with a credit card company you *must* have a record, a paper record. Never underestimate the value of paper in getting your problems solved. A copy of a letter is easy to show to a judge or jury. It is well known that while memories fade with time, a letter stays the same, as do notes of, say, a phone call. For this reason the American legal system loves people who state their complaints in writing. Keep written records of everything and always put your complaints in writing.

Also, when you send the credit card company a letter they often either lose it or ignore it. Or the company makes some sort of incorrect response and then throws your letter away. Company computer records then show that they had a "communication" from you on day X, but won't necessarily show what its contents were. The card companies think it is too expensive to keep their customers' letters on file. Since you have kept copies of your letters and the letters the credit card company sent you, you are in much better position to do battle than the company is. Just stick copies of those letters in your yearly bundle, right under the rubber band.

(If you are the file folder type, feel free to file away instead.)

---

### • CREDIT CARD INSIDER'S TIP •
### ON RECORD-KEEPING

1. Save all your bills and charge slips for at least a year. Six years is better.

2. Hang on to the envelopes, too, if they have a postmark date on them.

3. Write the date you get each bill or letter from a credit card company on the envelope and initial the note.

4. Keep copies of all letters the credit card companies send you and all letters you send them.

5. Keep those bills and letters in a rubber-banded bundle by year so you can find them when you need them.

6. Keep a list of all disputed amounts.

---

# 7

# How to Track Credit Card Company Errors

You need to keep track of the dollar amount of any and all errors on your bill. It is not as easy as you might think. You have to know what is disputed even after you have made a written complaint about the problems to the credit card company.

Why? Because, when you complain to the card company, it may not credit your account for the amount you say is wrong. The company does not *have* to do this, so that usually means it won't. The credit card companies got the law changed under the Reagan administration so that all they have to do is print on your statement something like "Do not pay any disputed amount."

*You* have to keep records to know how much the disputed items total. The federal Truth in Lending Act does not require the card companies to tell you how much the "disputed amount" is, or how many items the card company's records show as disputed, or how much interest is being added to your bill on disputed purchases—even though the card companies' computers could easily and cheaply do this.

That makes things mighty confusing for you if you do not have your own records. (Actually, I find it a bit confusing even *with* my own records). Some card companies seem to like to befuddle their customers. Perhaps these companies think a confused customer is less likely to complain, since he or she is having a hard time understanding what is going on.

The card company can continue to bill you for everything, including the disputed amount that the statement on your bill tells you not to pay. You can deduct the disputed amount, and the card company cannot tell credit bureaus you are delinquent in your payments (after all, you told the card company you do not owe the money you are not paying).

The card company can't try to collect the disputed sum, which means it can't sue you for it. But it can keep on billing you for it. Pretty silly, eh? But that is what the card companies got the Reagan guys at the Federal Reserve Board to okay.

To repeat, *you* are the one who must keep track so you know how much *not* to pay the credit card company. If you do not keep a record of disputed amounts you have no way to know what part of your bill not to pay. Knowing what *not* to pay is just as important as knowing what *should* be paid.

A Massachusetts Institute of Technology economist I met on the bus to Boston's Logan Airport had a Ph.D. in mathematical economics. Yet he had problems keeping track of the total of the disputed amount on billing errors on his card. He said that this drove him wild, as did the interest the card companies tacked onto his bill for money he did not owe. If Dr. M.I.T. had problems with this, what about the rest of us? Reform is needed. Congress should amend the law to require the card companies to print on each statement details about each unresolved disputed charge. (For information on groups working for reform you can join, see the Resources section.)

The credit card companies have giant computers and could certainly easily print that information on the bills. They refuse to do for

---

**• CREDIT CARD INSIDER'S TIP •**

Protect yourself on disputed amounts: pay the balance due, but subtract the total disputed amount, without subtracting the interest. This means you pay Killer Bank more than you really owe it, but you are safe from the bad effects of underpayment.

Better yet, pay off your account in full every month. You won't normally be billed for any interest. Then, if you have a dispute, you will know that any interest that shows up on your statement comes from the disputed amount. And you can deduct the interest from your payment just as you deduct the disputed amount.

their customers what they could so easily do. So until the law is changed you are going to have to do it all by yourself.

## Interest Charges on Disputed Amounts

The interest that the card company charges on disputed amounts is also—automatically—a disputed amount. That is only reasonable, since why should you pay interest on money you say you do not owe? But it means that the amount you do not legally have to pay changes with each statement.

Let's say a gourmet crook charged $553.43 to your account for a New Year's Day feast at Le Français. You have written to Killer Credit Corporation to let it know that this is definitely a billing error. You do not even like escargot, which you were billed for but never ate.

How do you know how much of the $83.46 interest/finance charges on your February statement from Killer Credit Corporation are tied to the crook's meal? Answer: You don't know.

In fact, you can't know, unless you are equipped to do some very complex mathematical calculations. The statement does not tell you how much of the interest Killer demands you pay you do not really owe. This is interest Killer knows it cannot legally do anything about collecting, but for which they continue to bill you. Yet if you estimate the disputed interest and make an error of just one penny, Killer could eventually, at the very least, report you as delinquent to a credit bureau.

On the next page is a form you can copy to keep track of the amounts you question on your credit card bills.

## SAMPLE DISPUTE RECORD FORM

Card Company Name _____

Account Number _____

| | |
|---|---|
| Merchant's name | |
| Amount disputed | |
| Date you notified card company of problem | |
| Date card company got notification | |
| Date card company responded | |
| Temporary credit to account (if yes, date and amount of credit) | |
| Problem resolution:<br>   Action and date<br>   Amount of final credit | |

# 8

# How to Complain About Fraudulent Charges and Mistakes on Your Account

Mistakes. Everybody makes 'em. Nobody likes 'em. But the credit card companies seem to make more than their share. And most of the companies do not seem to like to fix them.

They often don't like to straighten things out when the problem comes from a crook making illegal charges on your account. Better, some of the companies think, that you should pay for their mistakes or for crooked charges than that they should have to pay for them, which could very well happen if they can't get you to pay.

That is one reason Congress passed a law requiring the card companies to look into and correct errors, in which they defined "error" very broadly indeed. *Anything,* absolutely anything, you do not like about a credit card bill you get can be a billing error—if you say it is one. And calling it a billing error forces a card company to reasonably investigate the problem, if you follow the rules.

The federal Fair Credit Billing Act (a part of the Truth in Lending Act) was passed in the early seventies to protect you against the unscrupulous practices of credit card companies. Before the act was made law, according to *Give Yourself Credit*, a report of the U.S. House of Representatives: "You might have spent months or even years trying to straighten out your account if there was a mistake on your bill." Unfortunately, this can still happen, but the Fair Credit Billing Act does give you some clout. One of the most important things you can know about credit cards is how to use that clout.

The act sets up a required procedure for clearing up errors on your bills, a procedure that the card companies *must* follow or pay substantial bucks to you—if you know how to make them pay. The act also limits the amount of time a card company may take in getting back to you when you point out a billing error. If the card company does not follow the procedures established by this law for handling billing errors, you do not have to pay the company the amount in dispute whether you were right or wrong about the error, up to a maximum of $50.

Of course, if the card company does follow the law (wouldn't it be nice if this were more common than it is) and there is no billing error, then you have to pay the bill. You also still have to pay any amounts on your bill that you do not dispute as billing errors.

## What Is a Billing Error?

This is important stuff. A billing error turns out to be almost anything you question or don't like on your card statement. There is a billing error on your credit card account under federal law if the statement:

1. Lists a charge for something you did not buy.

   *Example:* There is a charge for $23.97 on your bill from the Westside Mambo Palace in Tango, Argentina. You don't mambo and have never been to Argentina.

2. Lists a charge and you cannot figure out what it is for.

   *Example:* There is a charge for $9.87 listed as "Merchandise #52NYNY," and you live in Des Moines and have never been to New York, New York. When you get a copy of the billing slip, you see that it is for a showerhead you bought at a local chain store. For some reason, it was processed as though it were bought at the chain's headquarters in New York.

3. Lists goods or services that were not accepted by you or by someone you asked to accept them (and "accepted" has a very broad and special meaning in the law that gives you all sorts of special protection).

   *Example:* You charge a squirt gun that won't squirt. You probably have not legally accepted the gun. For more on this example and a complete explanation of the powerful tool you have in this billing error rule, see Chapter 10.

**4.** Lists goods and services not delivered according to your deal with the seller.

> *Example:* You charge a new sofa to be delivered next Tuesday. It is not delivered until twelve Tuesdays later. Or it only lasts twelve weeks before collapsing. It was not delivered in accordance with your deal with the seller. Improper delivery is almost the same as item 3 above, nonacceptance.

**5.** Does not show correct credits for payments made, or goods returned.

> *Example:* You make a payment of $100 by mailing it to the right address on June 10. It arrives there June 12. The payment is not credited to your account until August 1, which means you get charged $5 in interest that would not have been due had the $100 been credited when it should have been credited. Both the failure to credit your account the day the payment arrived and the $5 charge for interest are billing errors.

> *Example:* You return a blender to the store on June 15. When the credit card statement arrives, dated August 1, the $32.50 price of the blender is not credited to your account. This failure to properly credit is a billing error. Another rule says returns must be credited to your account by the merchant within seven days of the return; failure to do so is a violation of the Truth in Lending Act by the merchant. The card company also has an obligation to promptly credit returns to your account.

**6.** Shows a mistake in arithmetic, including prices, finance charges, late payment charges, or any other charges.

> *Example:* You charge a shirt for $12.12, including tax. When the bill comes it is listed as $212.12. (The incorrect $5 interest charge in item 5 above could also fit into this category.)

**7.** Was not mailed or delivered to your current address, as long as the credit card company got written notice of your new address at least twenty days before the closing date of the statement.

*Example:* On May 1 the card company gets your written notice that your address has changed. On May 28 it closes your statement for the month and mails it to your old address. This is a billing error, even if the post office gallantly forwards the statement to your new place.

8. Just about anything on your bill that looks wrong to you. *If you call it a billing error in writing, the law says the credit card company must treat it as a billing error.* I repeat, if you *write* and say something is a billing error, it *is* a billing error.

## Fixing Billing Errors

In theory, to get a billing error repaired you write to the card company. You do this within sixty days of the mailing of the bill with the problem charge on it. In your letter you explain what you think is wrong.

The card company either fixes the problem within thirty days of getting your letter or writes back, telling you it has your letter and that it will investigate and resolve your problem within, at most, ninety days from the time it got your letter. Then it does investigate and does resolve your problem. If you don't agree with the resolution from the company you have ten days to write back and say you don't agree. If you do that, the company must notify you in writing of the identity of any credit reporting agencies it tells you are delinquent on that payment and must also tell the agencies that you dispute the charges. Card companies very rarely tell the agency that the charges are disputed; failure to do so is a violation of law.

Unfortunately the process doesn't always go this way. Banks exist to make profits, and following the legal rules may cut into those profits.

Now, let's look at how to really get billing error problems worked out.

First, to get the protection of the Federal Fair Credit Billing Act, *you must notify the card company* in writing *that there is a billing error on your account.* You do not legally have to use the phrase "billing error" in your letter, but I strongly recommend that you use it. I repeat, you *must* notify the card company *in writing* and you *should* use the phrase "billing error" in your letter.

The card company has to get your letter within sixty days of the time it mailed you the first statement containing the error. Here's an example:

> May 28—Card company mails your statement.
> June 1—Statement arrives at your house.
> July 28—You discover a $100 mistake on your May 28 statement.

You are too late (sixty-one days after the day the company mailed out the mistaken statement) to use your federal billing error correction rights. Of course, you would probably still want to write to the company and ask for a correction of the billing error. Though the company would not be legally required to correct the problem under federal billing error law, other provisions of the federal law might apply, and the laws of your state might give you rights above and beyond your federal rights. Also, most card companies are bound by various operating regulations of, for example, Visa U.S.A. and MasterCard International, which often require that card companies go beyond the legal requirements to resolve disputed items. Or the company might actually be interested in solving its customers' problems even if it is not legally required to do so.

> "A phone call—even numerous phone calls—may not be sufficient," warns the FDIC's Lisa Kimball. "I've seen several cases where people ended up responsible for fraudulent charges because they only notified the card issuer over the telephone."
> —Federal Deposit Insurance Corporation *Consumer News*

*Do not telephone!* If you telephone, you are in severe danger of losing all your legal rights. If the card company does not get *written* notice of a billing error within sixty days from the day it mailed you the incorrect bill, you are probably not protected by the federal billing error rules. (You might, however, have the right to go after the card company under state law or under other parts of federal law or those hidden operating regulations.)

Second, you have to send your letter to the proper address. This is probably not the same address you send your card payments to, but it could be. The card company gets to decide.

The way to tell where to send your letter is to look on your bill from the card company. There, the law says, you will find the address where the company wants you to send questions or billing error inquiries. It may be hard to find, printed in little blue type on the back of the statement perhaps, but it is required to be there. If you can't find the billing error address on your bill, call the card company and ask where on the statement it is hidden.

Third, in your letter put this information:

a. The account number, your name, your address, and the date of your letter
b. The statement that there is a billing error on your account
c. The reason that there is a billing error. For example, "The June 28, 2004 bill shows a charge of $563.56 for a TV I did not buy and know nothing about."

Some judges have said that even a penciled note scribbled on a credit card bill and sent to an address other than the one given on the bill is legal notice to a card company of a billing error. But why risk having to go to court on this question? Follow the suggestions above and avoid avoidable problems.

Fourth, *keep a copy of the letter* so that you have a record of what you sent. And note on your copy the date you mailed the letter.

## Keeping the Card Company from "Losing" Your Letter

You must have some way of *proving* that the card company got your letter. Many companies seem to make a habit of "losing" billing error and complaint letters from customers.

There are two ways to prove delivery. The cheapest and easiest is to send in a check as payment on your account along with your letter. Be sure to note on the front of the check "Enclosed with letter of June 33, 2002, to billing error department of Silly Bank." Note that a money order won't work. You do not get the paid money order back as you do a check. And note at the bottom of your letter something like "Check No. 1234 for $25.50 enclosed."

If you use this check method of proof, the card company does not have to credit payments made to your account at an address different from the address on the bill for payment for five days after it gets the check. (Checks sent to the usual payment address must be credited to your account the same day they are delivered.) So, if you are close to the payment deadline, you could incur a late fee.

Another possible problem is that the card company could "lose" your check and your letter, too. If it never cashes your check, you have no proof that it ever got your letter. This is rare, but it could and has happened.

In fact, even after the card company gets your letter and cashes the enclosed check, it may claim it never got the letter. I am aware of at least one case where the company claimed it never got the letter enclosed with the cashed check. After the consumer (who kept rather good records) complained rather seriously, got a lawyer, and filed suit, the card company, all the while claiming complete innocence, paid out around $20,000 to settle the case.

The second way to prove the company got your letter costs more than just mailing it in and involves a wait in line at the post office. It does provide absolute proof that you sent a letter and that the company got your letter.

Send the letter "certified mail—return receipt requested." You can get the two forms you need free at any post office. Be sure to staple to your copy of the letter the form that the postal clerk postmarks for you. Then do the same with the return receipt signed by a card company employee when it comes back to you in the mail a few days later.

The signed and dated return receipt is proof that the card company did get your billing error letter and of when it got it. It costs some extra to get that return receipt, but it's well worth it to have verification of delivery.

Where do faxes and E-mail fit into this? The Fair Credit Billing Act was written in the early seventies, before faxes were as common as toasters. And before E-mail was around at all. Notice *by mail* to the billing error address on your monthly statement is the way to go, even in the computer age—at least until the Truth in Lending Act is changed to accommodate advances in technology.

## The Disputed Amount—How Much Should You Make It?

While your dispute with the card company remains unresolved, you do not have to pay any of the disputed amount. The amount in dispute is the amount you tell the company is wrong, or the total amount of the questioned charge. For example, your account shows a charge for $100 from the Widget Store. You did charge something there, but it cost only $75. You tell the card company this in your letter. In this situation, the disputed amount is $25.

You could pay the undisputed $75. Or you could correctly claim that the entire $100 is a disputed amount and pay nothing now. Either is okay.

Or suppose the same $100 charge from the Widget Store appears on your account. But you do not recall ever buying anything from Widget. You tell the card company that you know nothing about the charge from Widget. The disputed amount is $100. You need pay nothing right now.

*Your Credit Limit and Disputed Amounts.* Even though you do not have to pay the disputed amount until the problem is worked out, the card company can still subtract the disputed sum from your credit limit. So if you dispute a $100 Widget charge you made and your credit limit is $1,000, you have only $900 worth of charging available on your account.

*Interest on Disputed Amounts.* If there is any error on the item you questioned, the company cannot charge you any interest on the total amount questioned for the whole time until the company resolves the problem. It does not matter if the error was the one you told the card company about or another one.

For example, you question the total $100 bill from the Widget Store. The card company investigates and finds that you did charge $99, not $100. It takes two months to find this out and correct your bill. It can't charge you any interest on either $100 or $99 for that time, even though you really owed nearly all the money. But if there was no error, the company can charge you for the interest while it was investigating the problem. Many companies do not try to recoup this interest because doing so tends to enrage the cardholder.

## After the Card Company Gets Your Letter

So the company has your letter and knows that you can prove the letter got to them. What happens next? Often, nothing. The company ignores your letter and hopes you will shut up and pay up. Yes, that is illegal. And yes, many card companies do it.

If the company ignores your letter, federal law clearly says it cannot collect the amount you claim is a billing error, up to $50. So if you contest a charge of $39.95 and the company doesn't respond within thirty days, it theoretically can't ever collect or even try to collect that $39.95. But the law fails to mention how you get it.

If the contested amount was, say, $56.98, you would have to pay $6.98 ($56.98 minus the $50 penalty). That penalty applies if the card company missed the thirty-day deadline, even if there was no billing error on your account. If there was a billing error on your account, of course, you would not have to pay the amount of the error.

Even if it turns out you really did owe the $39.95 (say, you forgot you charged all those drinks at Tipsy's Saloon), but the company did not respond to your letter within thirty days, you still do not have to pay any of the billed amount up to $50.

The $50 penalty is supposed to encourage the card companies to respond to your billing error letters as the law requires. But the law doesn't provide any special way to get your $50. The card company *should* credit it to your account automatically when they discover they have done you wrong. Since they are carefully ignoring your complaint, it is unlikely they are going to hand over the $50 without a push.

One approach is to send another letter to the company demanding that it immediately credit your account. Often that works.

But suppose the card company does obey the law. It finds it can't clear up your problem within thirty days. So it writes you to tell you it has your billing error letter and it will investigate your problem. That it will, after investigating, either credit your account for the amount you are contesting or tell you that you are wrong and that there is no error.

The time limit for correcting your bill is absolutely no more than *ninety* days—usually less. The company has to finally resolve your billing error problem within ninety days, or two billing periods from the time it gets your original letter, whichever is shorter. Of course, this doesn't mean it has to resolve it the way *you* want it resolved; it just means that the company can't drag it out past the legal time limits.

For example, your card bill is mailed to you on the first of each month. You get your June bill with an error in it on June 5. You find a mistake and send in a billing error letter on the fifteenth of June. The card company gets it on June 21. The company has seventy-two days (July and August have thirty-one days, which are added to the ten days from June 21 to June 30)—that is, until August 30—to reasonably investigate your problem and tell you, in writing, what its investigation found out. If it agrees with you that there is a billing error it must correct it within those seventy-two days.

Remember, the outside limit is ninety days. That doesn't mean ninety-one days. Also remember that the ninety-day limit applies only if you are billed less often than monthly—say, once every three months, something that was once done, but is now almost never seen. So, almost always, the time limit for billing error resolution is *less* than ninety days: usually, for folks who are billed monthly, something close to the seventy-two days as computed just above.

## What Is "Reasonable Investigation"?

The investigation the card company makes of your problem must be "reasonable." What a "reasonable" investigation consists of is not spelled out in the law. It surely means more than the company looking at its files and saying "We are right, you are wrong." This is too often the (illegal) response of card companies.

"A reasonable investigation may include contact with the merchant who honors a card, discussions with the consumer [that means you], and review of documentation," says the American Bankers' Association.

You do not have to show the bill is wrong. The card company has to show that the bill it sent you was right—if it can. And I don't think that failing to interview the merchant can be considered reasonable, although some card companies fail to do that interview.

There is another possibility. The card company finds that an error was made that you did not complain about. If this happens, it has to fix that error, too, even though you didn't complain about it. This might happen if the company has an internal audit and spots the error.

## Further Action You Can Take

What if the company does not properly correct the error? What happens if you do not agree with the result of the card company's investigation of a billing error? Or if the company sends you a letter full of gobbledy-gook that basically says, "We are right. You are wrong."

There are plenty of things you can do.

Suppose that you question a $100 charge. The card company, within the legal time limits, gets back to you and says that it has investigated and concluded that you owe it the $100. You know you did not make the charge. Do you legally have to pay? What should you do?

First, notify the card company *in writing* that the $100 is still disputed. You need to do this promptly after the company tells you that it has decided there was no error.

The law is fuzzy on what "promptly" means, but notice within ten days is certainly prompt according to the law. So you certainly have at least ten days from when you get the notice that the company claims you owe the disputed amount to write back and contest the claim. You might have as much as forty-five days.

When you send this prompt written notice that you still think you don't owe the disputed amount, you gain several things:

1. The company cannot report you as delinquent to any credit bureau unless it also reports that there is a dispute.
2. It must tell the credit bureau that you say you do not owe the disputed amount.
3. It must give you the name and address of anyone or any credit bureau it tells about your alleged debt.

That is it for the billing error procedure from the card company's end.

You, of course, can still file a complaint with the credit card cops (see Chapter 13); you can take the company to court; or you can just refuse to pay. But the card company can now try to collect the amount you say you do not owe.

Another thing to think about is sending a written complaint to the franchising Visa and MasterCard organizations who (theoretically at least) want to protect the value of their trademarks by making sure that the banks that issue the respective cards follow the law and the organization's operating regulations. These operating regulations often provide greater protection for the consumer than the law does; the regulations are often ignored by the card-issuing bank, but a complaint to Visa or MasterCard may get the bank to follow them due to pressure from on high. The address of the headquarters of both Visa and MasterCard are found in the Resources section.

Visa and MasterCard have at least somewhat different priorities than the issuing bank when you complain about billing error problems. The bank just wants you to shut up and pay up because otherwise the bank probably has to eat the disputed charges. Visa and MasterCard are more interested in keeping folks interested in carrying around and using credit cards. If folks can't get bad charges off their accounts, they might stop using cards to an extent an that would hurt the card business as a whole. Visa and MasterCard are also interested in preventing complaints to the government that might result in better, more effective regulation of the card industry. And someone who knows how to complain to Visa and MasterCard might just be the sort of person who knows how to complain to the credit card cops, or even worse, to Congress.

Unfortunately, the card companies do not make the operating regulations available to consumers, and in fact fight like crazy to keep them away from public view. If card users had access to the operating regulations, they might use them against the issuing banks. Nonetheless, a complaint to Visa or MasterCard may get your problem resolved under those shrouded operating regulations.

✍🏻

The whole billing error process does not provide a final resolution to your billing problem unless the card company agrees that there was a billing error. If it does not agree with you, you can fight on to get the error fixed.

Usually, though, the card company will have fixed most errors in the bills it sends you by this point in the procedure. After all, some of the most common problems are rather clearly billing errors, such as the billing of two identical charges for $96.28 at the same restaurant on the same date. Many times, the waiter runs the card through the card terminal twice, assuming that the first swipe didn't take. But it did, and you get billed for two expensive evenings when you had only one. The company should be able to resolve this sort of matter easily. Not that they always do.

Keep in mind that the billing error procedure is *not* meant to provide a legal decision on whether your bill was right or not. That is what courts are for in our legal system.

But the billing error procedure *is* meant to force the card company to take a serious look at your problem. Before the procedure was enacted into law, the card companies mostly just ignored customer complaints and problems and billed away for anything they felt like. Now, under pressure from the Truth in Lending Act–mandated billing error procedures and equivalent state laws, they are *slightly* better behaved.

## How to Complain Successfully

There are hundreds of thousands of jobs in this country held by people who are trained to cool you off, who are trained to tell you no in a variety of ways.

—Ralph Nader

To get satisfaction you may have to do some complaining.

Keep in mind that complaining is a learned art. You get better at it as you go along. If you do not start practicing, you will never be perfect. So when some wrong is done you, by a credit card company or anyone else, do something about it.

The essence of complaining is to get what you want. Otherwise, why complain? Don't do it to show the world you are right, or if there is nothing that the person or organization to whom you are complaining can do to set things right. Complain to those who have the power to solve the problem. Otherwise you are wasting your time.

Here is how to get a problem with your credit card statement resolved in the easiest, most effective way.

### Complaining Pointers

• *Complain in writing.* There is an old saying among lawyers: "If it's not in writing, it didn't happen." I've lost track of the number of aggravated consumers who have told me that they were promised on the phone that their problem would be solved, but who didn't write down who they talked to, what number they called, the date and time of the call, and what was said. You should be sure to keep a log of such information if you complain by phone; but it's much better to send a polite letter.

• *Nastiness gets you nowhere.* Being nasty, rude, or impolite to the person you are asking to help you may make you feel better. But it probably will not help you get your problem solved. In fact, it may seriously hinder your reaching any solution.

• *Do not start at the top.* If you start at the bottom, you just might get your problem solved right there. If you don't, you can move up the line (from customer service representative to supervisor to president) and have more opportunities to get what you want. If you go to the company president right off the bat, you cut down your chance of success. You can hardly expect a customer service representative to overrule the company president after the higher-ups have decided against you. But the president can easily overrule the negative decision of a customer service representative.

• *Fighting is hard work.* Some small things just may not be worth fighting about (unless you are *really* angry).

• *Know what you want.* Before you complain, have a clear idea of what it will take to solve the problem: a $12.83 credit; repair of your defective sofa; $500 and a letter of apology. If you do not know what you want, you are unlikely to get it.

• *"I have a problem, and I need your help."* This is a great line—especially effective in person. But use the basic idea even when you call or write. The thought is "I am a human being . . . and so are you."

• *"We have a problem."* We are working together to solve *our* problem. Make the person you want to help you your ally, working with you to solve your joint problem. *I* can help *you* solve our mutual problem. I can help you.

• *Someone else is the bad guy.* Do not be critical of the person you want to solve the problem. Make someone else the bad guy. "They" are the ones who caused the problems, not the person you are dealing with.

• *BE PERSISTENT.* Many (if not most) credit card companies hope that you will just go away if they give you a hard time. Do not let these tactics work. Give them a harder time in return. Don't drop your complaint.

• *Be brief.* Almost always a one-page, typewritten letter is enough. Two pages should be the outside limit unless your problem is really extraordinarily complex.

• *Give a deadline.* If someone at the card company promises you something—say, a photocopy of your statement—get a date by which you should have it. For anything important, follow up with a letter along the lines of "Dear Mr. Card: Just a note to confirm our conversation today in which you told me I would get a copy of my statement by June 23." Or when you write, close with a statement such as: "Please be so kind as to have your response to this letter in my hands by July 23." Generally you should pick a date at least ten days or so in the future. It is also a good idea to check the calendar so that you don't demand that the reply be in your hands on a Sunday.

---

Brian McConnell, president of Commonwealth Multimedia, a company that writes software for automated phone systems, was frustrated. He couldn't get a real person to answer the phone at First Union Bank of Virginia and deal with his complaint.

Finally he wrote a program that phoned automatically eight Union Bank numbers with a recording that said something to the effect of: "This is an automated customer complaint. To hear a live complaint press 27." Anyone pressing 27 heard: "The customer is unable to come to the phone right now, but your call is very important to him. Thank you for being patient." The message went on and on, finally giving McConnell's name and telephone number.

Mr. McConnell was perturbed because he had unsuccessfully tried to reach someone at Union's headquarters to report an ATM problem.

First Union apologized to McConnell.

—from an Associated Press
dispatch in the *Los Angeles Times*

---

• *Type your complaint.* I wish I could tell you that a handwritten letter on notebook paper gets the same attention as a beautiful computer-printed letter on watermarked rag bond from Tiffany's. But it ain't so. If you can't type or use a computer to print your letter you will be best off getting someone to do the letter for you.

• *Never ever send originals of documents.* Keep the originals of all letters from the company, credit card slips, statements, and all documents. If you send them to the company they could get "lost"—and your case along with them. Document "loss" is a big problem with credit card companies. Some think it is easier to "lose" documents than to solve problems.

### The Complaint Letter

Every good complaint has six parts:

1. A statement of the problem: "My card bill is incorrect."
2. The facts (lawyers are told that the statement of the facts is the most important part of a case): "My card bill shows a purchase of a Super Byzantium computer for $3,987.56 at Wicky-Wacky Computing on April 15. In fact, all I bought there was an IBM typewriter ribbon for 98¢."
3. What you want: "Please immediately credit my account for the $3,986.58 difference."
4. The deadline: "Please respond to this letter by June 10." Two weeks or so might be a reasonable amount of time to allow.
5. The threat: "I hope that we will be able to immediately resolve this problem, so that no further action will be required."
6. The polite close: "Thank you for your anticipated help in solving this problem."

Make sure that your complaint letter has these six parts and you will have your best shot at getting corrective action.

Remember: Be nice, be polite, be persistent. Complain in writing.

## Fraud and Errors on Business Card Accounts (You Are Not Protected with Business Cards)

Now that you know about some of your rights as a card user you might assume that these rights apply to all credit cards. Not so.

The card companies have figured out a very clever way to get small-business people to give up many of their credit card rights and much of their credit card power. Just tell 'em that the card company is going to give 'em a special business card that will (somehow) be really great, very superior as well as highly prestigious. Forget to mention that a business card user gives up his or her incredibly useful, incredibly valuable stop-payment and billing error dispute rights. Just keep telling the potential business card applicant how superior that business card will be (and don't mention the loss of those precious rights).

How do you lose your valuable credit card rights? It's right in the law. The credit card rights I discuss in this book protect individual consumers, not businesses. If a consumer uses a small-business card, not a regular consumer-type card, he loses *all* the hard-won rights and protections of the consumer credit card.

In fact, the U.S. Supreme Court has said so. In a 1981 case called *Koerner v. American Express* (452 U.S. 233), the Court held that folks using business cards give up a whole pile of rights.

American Express issued credit cards to John E. Koerner and Co., Incorporated, including one for the use of Louis Koerner, an officer of the corporation, but made Mr. Koerner sign an agreement that he would be liable along with the corporation for all the charges on the corporate card he carried. American Express looked into the corporation's credit rating, but not Mr. Koerner's.

Ten years later, a dispute over $55 in American Express charges for flight insurance and annual fees, apparently automatically billed to the Koerner Company account, came up. After many complaints, American Express apparently finally did credit the account for most of the disputed $55, after the corporation refused to pay.

Then, about a year later, Mr. Koerner tried to charge a plane ticket for a business trip. The ticket agent told him that he had to talk to the American Express employee who was on the line and he was told by American Express that his card was canceled because payment was delinquent. The Amex worker told the ticket agent to cut the card in two and give it back to Mr. Koerner.

Mr. Koerner filed a lawsuit against American Express, saying that the card had been canceled in retaliation for the company's complaints. The case made it to the Fifth Circuit Court of Appeals, which said that, since Mr. Koerner had agreed to pay the bill if the Koerner company did not, American Express had to follow the billing error rules. "If [American Express] can recover from a consumer, then it must abide by the requirements of [the Truth in Lending Act] for correction of billing errors in a consumer's credit card statement. The card company cannot have it both ways. . . ." This was a sensible decision which protected the rights of an individual card user, even if the card was a company card.

Amexco was apparently unhappy with the Fifth Circuit's decision because it didn't want to have to follow consumer protection law on business accounts, so Amexco took the matter to the Supreme Court. The Supreme Court decided that Mr. Koerner was out of luck. Accounts used primarily for business purposes, even if the card company can go after the individual user for payment, are not covered by the consumer protections of the Truth in Lending Act. Mr. Koerner had been able to identify only seven nonbusiness charges on the card over four years and, said the Supreme Court, if the card is not opened for consumer purposes and not used for mostly consumer purposes, then forget about consumer protection. Tough luck, Mr. Koerner, and anybody else who has a problem on their business card.

It's interesting to ask *why* business cards aren't covered. The idea is apparently that businesses can negotiate a good deal and special terms on contracts with a card company, but the consumer is not able to do this, not having the extra financial clout, or, say, a lawyer on retainer. However, only the biggest corporations are really in a position to negotiate special deals. Somehow, I have a tough time imagining Faye's Flowers of Highland Park, Inc., negotiating a good deal with American Express when it responds to the mail solicitation for a corporate card Faye can use when she goes to the flower show in New Orleans. The Supreme Court should have made a different decision, following what the Fifth Circuit did. But it didn't. So Congress should change the law to protect *all* card users, but don't hold your breath.

In the meantime what's a poor business card user to do? One self-protection tactic is to not use the company card if you can help it. Put all charges on your personal card and use it lots at the grocery store, the drugstore, and everywhere else you make what are clearly consumer purchases.

Another tactic is to be sure that the company that gets you the card is sharp enough to negotiate billing error and other protections into its deal with the card company (good luck!). I personally think that a law that requires a small business, or even a pretty big business, to negotiate special terms in its deal with a card company in order to have the most minimal protections is a law that needs to be changed.

Meanwhile, look out for business card solicitations in the mail. And don't accept those business card offers unless you want to give up your credit card rights.

# Billing Error Correction Correspondence from Start to Successful Finish

This chapter has been included here because lots of folks have a tough time figuring out how to respond to the card companies' sometimes evasive tactics.

Read through the following correspondence for an example of how a billing error may be successfully corrected by you, the card user. Then take a look at my comments following the letters.

999 Consumer Lane
On-Top-of-Things, CA 99999
September 3, 2001

Continental Excess Company
Customer Service Dept.
666 Continental Excess Expressway
Buncum, FL 66666

RE: Account No. 123456789

Dear Continental Excess:

I wish to call your attention to a billing error on my recent statement dated August 23. In regard to reference No. KQZ2283J, Superbreak Mini-London, I did not receive this service, and it was billed in error.

A reservation was made by phone on July 2 and canceled by phone on July 4.

Very sincerely yours,
A. GoodWoman

Continental Excess Company
666 Continental Excess Expressway
Buncum, FL 66666
September 12, 2001

ACCOUNT NUMBER: 123456789

Dear Ms. GoodWoman:

To assist SUPERBREAK MINI in investigating your recent reservations claim, please complete the accompanying form and send it to us in the enclosed return envelope.

While waiting for this matter to be resolved, we are issuing a temporary credit for $108.45 to your account. Unless we receive the above item from you by September 29, 2001, however, we will remove the temporary credit and charge your account again.

We appreciate your help in resolving this situation quickly.

If you have any questions, or if we can be of further service, please call us at the telephone number on your statement.

Sincerely,
R. Willard
Claims Research Representative

*[as filled in by Ms. GoodWoman]*

Continental Excess Company
666 Continental Excess Expressway
Buncum, FL 66666

CANCELLATION INFORMATION

CANCELLATION DATE: July 4 by phone from Paris

CANCELLATION TIME: 6 P.M. Paris time

CARDHOLDER'S CANCELLATION TIME ZONE: 6 P.M. Paris

CANCELLATION NUMBER: Not applicable

PLEASE CHECK BELOW TO INDICATE WHICH OF THE FOLLOWING DOCUMENTS YOU HAVE TO SUPPORT YOUR CLAIM. BE SURE TO ATTACH COPIES.

__ hotel bill

__ hotel bill incurred at alternative location

— canceled check or the advance deposit receipt

— receipt for taxi fare (or specify amount)

— phone charge incurred in the move (or specify amount)

— telephone bill verifying the cancellation—include the name of the person you spoke to

## ADDITIONAL INFORMATION

reservation phone #: <u>01-2789-99999</u>

reservation made through: <u>not applicable</u>

date reservation made: <u>July 2—phone call from Paris</u>

confirmation number: <u>not applicable</u>

date reserved for: <u>July 6</u>

— If necessary, please use the reverse side to briefly explain or clarify any of the above information.

This reservation was canceled by telephone from Paris using a Telecarte from a pay phone on July 4. This charge was billed in error, as I did not stay at a hotel that Superbreak Mini booked. I suggest that Superbreak Mini try to show proof of my having registered at a hotel booked by them. Also I wrote all this in my letter of Sept. 2 and find this form just an additional inconvenience.

A. GoodWoman

Continental Excess Company
666 Continental Excess Expressway
Buncum, FL 66666
October 18, 2001

ACCOUNT NUMBER: 123456789

Dear Ms. GoodWoman:

In September 2001 we issued a temporary credit to your Card Account for $108.45 and told you we would research your claim with SUPERBREAK MINI.

As the enclosed explanation/itemization will show, the charge(s) were correct. We are therefore removing the temporary credit(s) and charging your account again. The adjustment(s) will appear on an upcoming statement.

If you have any questions, or if we can be of further service, please call us at the telephone number on your statement.

Sincerely,
R. Willard
Claims Research Representative

Enclosed with this letter was a copy of a form from Conexco sent to SuperBreak, which stated:

Our Cardmember has queried the attached charge for which we have already paid you. We have been notified that the accommodation was canceled prior to the original reservation date. Therefore, we would be pleased if you will investigate this claim and advise us of your findings to enable us to resolve this query, on your behalf, with the Cardmember.

SuperBreak filled out the form with the claim:

Our booking conditions state that cancellations must be made in writing before the date of travel. No letter of cancellation was received; therefore no refund is due.

999 Consumer Lane
On-Top-of-Things, CA 99999
November 6, 2001

Mr. Edward Steelman, Vice President
Consumer Card Division, Continental Excess Company
100 Folderol Street
New York, NY 00000

RE: Account No. 123456789

Dear Vice President Steelman:

I am writing to you about a billing error on my Conexco account. I have been unable to resolve this matter with your customer service people.

In July of this year a reservation was made with SuperBreak Mini Holidays in London, England, by telephone. The cost was to be charged to my Conexco account.

Two days later, I called SuperBreak, several days before the day for which the reservation was made, and canceled it.

The cancellation was accepted and no mention of any further action required on my part was made by SuperBreak.

Nonetheless, a charge for $108.45 appeared on my account.

I queried this as a billing error and received a reply stating that SuperBreak requires all cancellations to be in writing and that Conexco would continue to charge my account for the $108.45.

This is wrong. I properly canceled this reservation in exactly the same fashion in which it was made, and it was accepted by the vendor.

I have consulted my attorney about this matter, and he advises me that Conexco has not complied with applicable federal and California law, and that I may file a complaint with the Federal Trade Commission and also file a lawsuit.

I would prefer to avoid this. Please have this incorrect charge for $108.45 removed permanently from my account so that this matter may be closed.

I did not receive the goods and services for which I am being charged.

I do not owe and will not pay the $108.45.

I would appreciate a reply to this letter by November 26, 2001.

Thank you for your anticipated help in resolving this problem.

Very sincerely yours,
A. GoodWoman

Interestingly, on November 22, Ms. GoodWoman received not one but two letters from Conexco, both in envelopes addressed to her. But one was to a Mr. Giventherunaround she had never heard of.

Continental Excess Company
100 Folderol Street
New York, NY 00000
November 19, 2001

Dear Mr. Giventherunaround:

Thank you for writing to me personally about the difficulty with your account. Like you, I am extremely upset about the length of time this dispute has gone unresolved.

Since your account is serviced out of our Southern Regional Operations Center in Buncum, Florida, I have asked Mr. John Doe, Senior Vice President, Operations, to investigate this problem immediately. I will personally follow this up with Mr. Doe until it is resolved.

I am intensely interested in any situation which reflects on the Continental Excess reputation for service. We will make every effort to restore your confidence in us.

Sincerely,
Edward Steelman,
Vice President, Consumer Card Division

Continental Excess Company
100 Folderol Street
New York, NY 00000
November 19, 2001

Dear Ms. GoodWoman:

Thank you for writing to me personally about the difficulty with your account. Like you, I am extremely upset about the length of time this dispute has gone unresolved.

Since your account is serviced out of our Southern Regional Operations Center in Buncum, Florida, I have asked Mr. Robert Roe, Senior Vice President, Operations, to investigate this problem immediately. I will personally follow this up with Mr. Roe until it is resolved.

I am intensely interested in any situation which reflects on the Continental Excess reputation for service. We will make every effort to restore your confidence in us.

Sincerely,
Edward Steelman,
Vice President, Consumer Card Division

Next, on November 28, Ms. GoodWoman received a letter dated November 13, claiming it was to resolve a billing error inquiry she had never made and knew nothing about.

Continental Excess Company
666 Continental Excess Expressway
Buncum, FL 66666
November 13, 2001

ACCOUNT NUMBER: 123456789

Dear Ms. GoodWoman:

You recently inquired about an error on your statement.

We have made the necessary adjustment(s) and credit(s) of $49.87 appear(s) on your November 2001 statement.

If you have any questions, or if we can be of further service, please call us at the telephone number on your statement.

Sincerely,
R. Willard
Claims Research Representative

Continental Excess Company
1234 Washington Drive
Firery, AZ 66666
December 3, 2001

ACCOUNT NUMBER: 123456789

Dear Ms. GoodWoman:

At the request of Mr. Steelman, I am writing concerning the difficulty you have had with your account.

By now, you will have received a letter from our Customer Service Department advising you that a credit of $49.87 had been issued to your account and a $58.58 credit had been received from SuperBreak Mini Holidays. The $49.87 credit appeared on the November statement. However, a review of the account indicates that the $58.58 credit on the October statement was from Macy's and not from SuperBreak Mini Holidays. Therefore, an adjustment has been issued to credit your account for the $58.58. This credit will appear on the December statement.

Thank you for taking the time to write and bring this matter to our attention. We have valued your card membership since 1979 and look forward to serving your future card needs.

Sincerely,
J. Holiday

Ms. GoodWoman is still a little bemused by all this correspondence, but she says: "They finally did credit me for the $108.45 and I don't really care if they say it came from Macy's or wherever as long as I finally got the right amount of credit. What a pain in the neck, though!"

Use the card user's letters as models for you if you encounter a billing error. In the correspondence above you will see that Conexco made two obvious errors in dealing with this simple customer problem.

In the letter of November 13 it confused one charge with another and claimed that a credit of $49.87 had been made by SuperBreak when it had not. And it sent two almost identical letters dated November 19 to its customer. One was addressed to her, the other to a gentleman living over a thousand miles away. Even in dealing with this not-so-complex problem we find two card company errors. This is typical of what I find in dealing with card companies.

You may want to get the name of the card company's big shot. That name is useful, as you have seen in the correspondence above, when you have a problem which you have a tough time getting resolved. The names of credit card company big shots can usually be found in the annual reports of publicly owned card companies, free from the respective corporate headquarters. Or call the card company's toll-free 800 number for your area and ask for the name and address of the current president, or if you want the annual report, for the corporate headquarters address and telephone. There is no need to mention just why you want the annual report or the big shot's name and address when you request it. Or, look the company up in a banking directory at the reference department of your local library. Reference librarians are great pals for folks looking into credit card matters.

### Get Lost, Buddy—The Pattern of Card Company Responses to Customer Problems

It is interesting to see in these letters the pattern I have seen over and over again. First the card company asks for more information "to investigate." Then it writes back saying, "Sorry, you must pay." Then, if the card user persists, perhaps complains to higher-ups, credit is given on the account. In other words, the legal rights of the card user are ignored by most card companies unless the card user is more aggressive than most in getting problems fixed. There is no real concern on the part of most card companies for the legal rights of their customers. Only those who look as though they might fight back get their legal rights.

Perhaps this "Get lost, buddy" attitude toward customers helps explain why American banks are finding it more and more difficult to compete against Japanese-owned banks now operating in the United States. Japanese-owned banks are said to be very concerned about the correctness of their relationships with their customers, and are interested in treating them with courtesy, respect, and politeness.

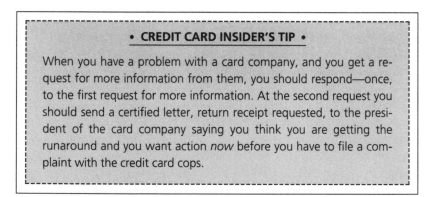

• **CREDIT CARD INSIDER'S TIP** •

When you have a problem with a card company, and you get a request for more information from them, you should respond—once, to the first request for more information. At the second request you should send a certified letter, return receipt requested, to the president of the card company saying you think you are getting the runaround and you want action *now* before you have to file a complaint with the credit card cops.

# 10

## Stop Payment on Your Credit Card: Your Super-Powerful Anti-Rip off Weapon

This chapter on your credit card stop-payment rights just might be the most important consumer information on credit cards you'll ever see. Stopping payment is an incredibly powerful weapon against rip-offs that you have as a credit card user. This weapon can save you *lots* of money and protect your consumer rights in many, many situations.

Have you ever been dissatisfied with something you paid for by credit card? Who hasn't? Would you like to get your money back even months after you paid the bill? Who wouldn't? You will find out how to do just that in this chapter.

Keep in mind that stopping payment on your credit card is *not* like stopping payment on a check. It's much better from the consumer's point of view, because it's powerful and cheaper. Keep in mind that the stop-payment rights discussed here don't apply to debit cards. Your stop-payment right does apply to all *credit* cards, be they store cards, American Express Cards, Visa cards, MasterCards, or phone company credit cards.

What is supposed to happen after you give the credit card company a stop-payment notice? You have two kinds of stop-payment rights under the federal Truth in Lending Act. I call them the good-faith stop and the sixty-day stop.

In the case of the good-faith stop, giving written notice to the "in case of problems or disputes" address on your monthly bill should be the end of the matter. The credit card company should remove the charge from your account. The card company should not tell you it needs more information or that it is "investigating" the matter (though it probably will tell you that).

Your good-faith stop-payment right, except for possible limitations that will be discussed later, is absolute. That is, it does not depend on any additional information given to or correspondence with the card company. There should be no hold put on your credit limit.

The matter should be left to you and the merchant to settle. Essentially, you should be in the same place you would be if you had stopped a check because you were unhappy with something you had bought. That's not always what happens, though. I'll discuss how to deal with problems in the process later on. For now, here's an example of how things are supposed to go.

### How Stop Payment Should Work

Charlie and his lady were on vacation in San Diego, almost 900 miles from their home in the Northern California logging town of Eureka. The transmission in their '79 Chrysler went out. The car was towed into a franchised transmission shop, Sick Trans, not too far from the Mexican border.

There Mr. Trick quoted them $598 for a complete overhaul and re-build of the transmission. Charlie didn't know anything about transmissions. But he sure knew he needed the car to get home. He told Trick to go ahead.

The final bill presented was $798. "You needed a new set of right-handed doohickies," said Trick. "Cost two hundred more than I thought." Charlie sighed, put the $798 on his Visa card, and headed back to Eureka.

In Eureka he asked Fred, his old reliable mechanic, to take a look at the transmission. He was shocked to hear Fred say, "Nobody's done any work on this transmission, at least not for the last few thousand miles or so. Looks like they just put some fluid in it and washed it off."

Charlie was shocked. He was honest in his work and expected other folks to be the same. Then he got mad. But what could he do? San Diego was a long way off. The amount of money involved was certainly not enough to make it worth his while to hire a lawyer. And Charlie really could not justify an 1,800-mile round-trip journey back to San Diego on the off chance he could get a refund from Sick Trans. Was there anything Charlie could do?

If Charlie had paid the $798 in cash he would probably have had to just forget his loss. He would have had to do the same if he had paid by check unless—unlikely!—the check had not been immediately cashed and so had not yet cleared Charlie's bank by the time he heard the bad news from Fred. Luckily for Charlie, he had paid with his Visa card, and had bought a copy of this book. He knew what to do.

He sent a letter off to Sick Trans telling them that he was unhappy with their "services," and why. He demanded a refund. Then when his Visa bill came in from the bank he sent off a letter (certified mail, return receipt requested) to the bank at the special address printed (in tiny type) on the bill under "in case of errors or questions about your bill."

Charlie's letter to the bank is shown below. In it he makes the essential legal points.

123 Logging Road
Eureka, California
March 14, 1999

Big Bucks Bank Customer Service Division
P.O. Box 666
Rotten Falls, South Dakota

RE: Card account #1234567890

Dear Customer Service Folks:

This letter concerns the charge for $798.00 from Sick Trans in San Diego that appears on my card statement dated February 13, 1999. The alleged work was not done and I want you to charge back to your vendor, Sick Trans, the $798.00 charged. This total charge is a billing error. It is also a charge-back demand.

I have contacted the merchant, Sick Trans, in a good-faith attempt to resolve the dispute and have been unable to so resolve it.

Please see to it that my account is immediately credited with the $798.00 I was charged.

Sincerely yours,
Charlie Goodguy

Certified Mail No. P-123 456 789—Return Receipt Requested

The bank charged back the $798 to Sick Trans's account with its bank in San Diego, removed the charge from Charlie's next bill, and, at least from Charlie's point of view, that was that.

Charlie felt much better.

Of course this left Mr. Trick tearing his hair out. Sick Trans *could* sue Charlie in court for the $798, but its chances of winning and collecting are small. It probably won't do anything. Or Sick Trans's bank could refuse to accept the charge-back. But in this situation the chances of that are, I think, small, because Charlie has a good and reasonable case.

Consumer Action, a San Francisco–based group, says that the credit card stop-payment remedy is so useful for the consumer that many of the most dishonest car repair shops have stopped taking credit cards. You might want to keep this in mind the next time you need to choose a garage to work on your car. If a garage does not take credit cards, look out!

### The Good-Faith Stop Payment

What Charlie did in the example just above was to use some of his rights under the federal Truth in Lending Act. The act says that if you use your credit card to buy something in your home state or within 100 miles of your billing address (as discussed below, there are some interesting issues about just what that 100 miles means) that costs more than $50 (again, there are interesting issues about just where the $50 comes in), you can stop payment. You just tell the credit company not to pay the bill.

The geographic and "must be more than $50" limits do not apply if the card company sent you a solicitation to buy the thing you are unhappy with, or if the card company or someone working with the card company sold it to you. Suppose, for example, you bought the flying suitcase advertised in your credit card bill ("Why carry your suitcase when it can fly behind you as you walk unencumbered through the airport?") and, unfortunately, the motor in your particular flying suitcase won't get it off the ground.

Before telling the credit card company to stop payment, you have to make a good-faith effort to work out the problem with the merchant. That good-faith effort can be (and is) as simple as calling up to say, "Mr. Trick, I am not satisfied with the services and goods I bought from you. I want a refund." Or it can be as elaborate as sending a letter via certified mail, return receipt requested, telling why you are dissatisfied and want your money back. A telephone call, a letter, a visit to the store—all are okay under part of the law. Your notification to the seller of just how unhappy you are does not have to be made in writing. And there is no definition in the law of just what "good faith" means.

However, it is a good idea to notify the credit card company in writing that you have made a good-faith effort to work out the problem with the merchant and that it has not been worked out. You are not required by law to do this, but it does make things very clear. Your good-faith effort to resolve things with the merchant, when you tell him orally or in writing that you are not satisfied, is enough, legally, to trigger a stop payment.

However, suppose you did not write to the credit card company about your unhappiness before you paid the bill. But you did tell *either* the merchant or a credit card company representative, over the phone or in person, before you paid the bill for the problem purchase. Then you have met the law's notice requirement for a good-faith stop payment. Written notification to the card company is a good idea. It is not a legal requirement.

This is very important. You do not have to give written notice, no matter what the card company claims. Thus, in *Montgomery Ward v. Horgan* (448 Atlantic 2nd 15), a 1982 Vermont case, a phone call and notes written on payment stubs were held by the judge to be a reasonable effort to give notice, even though Ward claimed (surprise!) that it had no record of any complaints.

*Example:* You stay at Quiet Haven Hotel in Shady Rest, Connecticut, on your way home to Hartford. As you check in, you ask the clerk, "Is it really quiet here at night? I have to get a good night's sleep." "Like a tomb," the clerk replies as he takes the imprint of your credit card.

The graveyards must be mighty lively in Shady Rest. The local four-on-the-floor, eight-barrel carburetor, all-night drag strip is right next to your room, and the airport take-off pattern for jets is two hundred feet from it. When you check out, you tell the clerk, "It was really noisy here last night. I am not satisfied with the room. Please do not charge my credit card account."

The clerk tells you that would be "against company policy." He will have to charge your account.

Four months later, after you have paid the credit card bill, you read this book and find out about your stop-payment rights. Your conversation with the desk clerk, *even though you have already paid the bill*, is notice enough to enable you to get your money back from the credit card company! Of course, the card company may not be eager to acknowledge this legal principle and may even tell you that it's not so.

### Limits on the Good-Faith Stop Payment

You may not be able to use the good-faith stop payment for purchases made outside the state of the billing address on your credit card account. Or, if outside your home state, more than 100 miles from your billing address. Or for purchases of less than $50. (If this is a bit confusing, read on.) Why can't you use a good-faith stop when the purchase was made for less than $50, outside the state where your billing address is located, or more than 100 miles from your billing address? There is no *good* reason.

These limits were picked up by Congress from California's Song-Beverly Credit Card Act of 1971. Song-Beverly was one of the first laws to deal with the rampant crookedness displayed by some credit card companies in the late sixties and early seventies. The bill's authors, Song and Beverly, apparently thought that since this was a state law, the stop-payment provision should apply only within a certain California sphere of influence.

Perhaps S & B were right then, but there was and is no good reason to have these limits in a federal law. The reasons usually given for still having these limits are that the credit card company can somehow police dishonest merchants near to it, but that it cannot do this for a bad merchant who is far away; and when you buy something for less than $50 with a credit card, it is somehow really a cash transaction. Neither one of these rationales is rational.

Today, huge credit card companies shoot applications, and have representatives, all over the nation. Also, the card company, no matter where it is, has the power to charge back problem charges to the merchant and take the money right out of the merchant's bank account. Plus, with many, if not most card users having accounts with credit card companies hundreds of miles away, the idea of the local customer buying from the little store up the street, with a credit card issued by the banker on the corner, is way out of date. So are the limits on your good-faith stop-payment rights.

### No Time Limit on the Good-Faith Stop

How long do you have to tell either the merchant or the credit card company that you are not satisfied? There is no time limit given in the Truth in Lending Act.* I emphasize: There is *no* time limit on your right to get your money back from a seller, or a credit card company, once you have tried in good faith to work out a problem. The actual complaint to the seller crystallizes then and there your right to stop payment.

Even if you go ahead and pay the bill *after* complaining to *either* the seller or the credit card company, you can still stop payment, even months later, and get your money back. That is the law, no matter what credit card companies or merchants may tell you. Once you have complained to either the credit card company or the merchant, you have a right to stop payment not limited by any time period at all.

Theoretically, you could tell a stereo store the day after you bought a laser disc player that you did not think it was up to snuff. Then three or eight years later you could tell the credit card company you wanted your money back and get it. Of course, there might be a bit of yelling by the card company. And a judge might think you had behaved unreasonably. Judges often don't like unreasonable people. So don't wait three or eight years to exercise your right to the good-faith stop.

According to the Federal Reserve Board, if the merchant has gone bankrupt before you can complain, you don't have to make any complaint to the merchant before exercising your good-faith stop-payment rights.

### Complain Before You Pay the Card Company

You have to make the problem known to either the merchant or the credit card company *before* you pay the credit card company's bill for the thing you are dissatisfied with. Otherwise you may get involved with the Federal Reserve Board's silly allocation rule I will tell you about later in this chapter. You could even lose all your rights to make a good-faith stop payment. And you certainly do not want that to happen.

---

*See, for example, 15 United States Code, section 1666i and Federal Reserve Board Regulation Z, section 226.12(c).

---

**• CREDIT CARD INSIDER'S TIP •**

"Complain before you pay" is the rule to remember when paying credit card bills. It is always best to complain in writing, but an oral complaint to the merchant can be enough.

---

*A How-To Example.* Debbie used her National Express Card, at a travel agent's near her Chicago home, to pay $2,453 for a trip for herself and her husband to Jamaica. It was to be, according to the brochure, "six nights, seven days of tropical luxury, in a two-room honeymoon suite, all meals included." When Deb and her husband got to the hotel, they discovered that it was still under construction. The elevator to their sixth-floor room did not work, so they had to walk up and down several times a day in un-air-conditioned temperatures of ninety-plus degrees. They also discovered that the two-room "honeymoon suite" consisted of a bedroom on the sixth floor and a conference room on the second floor. The manager pointed out, when they complained, that the brochure did not say the two rooms of the "suite" would be connecting or even on the same floor! And finally, the meals included were served, allegedly due to the unfinished state of the hotel kitchen, in a rather dumpy restaurant two miles from the hotel. No transportation provided. "An easy walk," said the desk clerk.

Deb and her husband complained to the manager but got no satisfaction. They wrote down his name and when and how they had complained, and stuck it in their "vacation problems" envelope. They complained to the travel agent when they got back to Chicago but got no satisfaction. They wrote down his name and when and how they had complained, and stuck it in their "vacation problems" envelope. They complained to the service representative at the other end of the credit card company's 800 phone line and got no satisfaction. They wrote down his name and when and how they had complained, and stuck it in their now-bulging envelope.

They could not afford to hire a lawyer, although they thought about it. So they decided that, to protect their credit rating, they would have to pay the $2,453 that had shown up on Deb's credit card bill, and they did. Then three months later, they got this book and discovered that they could get their $2,453 back.

They sent the complaint letter you will find below to the credit card company, and lo and behold, on next month's statement appeared a credit for $2,453!

However, they would have been in an even stronger position if they had used their stop-payment rights *before* paying the bill. It is *always* easier to keep your money than it is to get it back after you have paid it out.

100 East Armitage Avenue
Chicago, Illinois
June 35, 2001

National Express Company Customer Service
666 National Express Expressway
Mousetown, Florida 66666

Dear Customer Service Folks:

This letter is about my account #1234567890.

It concerns the charge for $2,453.00 from Island Fantasy Vacations that appears on my bill for March of this year.

I was not satisfied with the goods and services provided and attempted in good faith to resolve the matter with Mr. Mean, the manager at IFV on February 30 and with Mr. Cruel, the desk clerk at IFV, on February 31. We also complained to Mr. Nono of your customer service department on February 39, after our return from the completely unsatisfactory trip we took with IFV.

In accord with my rights under the federal Consumer Credit Protection Act, please credit my account with the sum of $2,453.00 and charge back this sum to IFV. Please also consider this charge to be a billing error.

Thank you for your anticipated help.

Sincerely,
Debbie Justice

Certified Mail # P 123-456-789—Return Receipt Requested

### The 100-Mile Limit

How far is 100 miles? A whole lot farther than you might think. Suppose you buy a gold-plated wuzzy over 100 miles from your billing address and outside your home state. Then you find out that the wuzzy won't wuz. You need to stop payment on the charge. But you bought your wuzzy too far away for the good-faith stop to work. Or did you?

Legally, the place where a thing was bought is often not really clear. What if you call a SuperBigNational store near your Boston home for information on a wuzzy and that SBN store does not have the information? They have a branch of SBN in Las Vegas call you with the needed info. And the Vegas office takes your order. The Las Vegas office takes your MasterCard number so it can bill your account $88.88 for the wuzzy, which will be shipped and billed from Omaha.

Then two weeks later, the wuzzy is shipped in from Nebraska and you pick it up, as agreed, at the Boston store, two blocks from home. You take it home, only to discover that the wuzzy will not wuz.

When you return to SuperBigNational's Boston store to complain, you are told that you broke the thing and cannot have a refund. "Wuz off," they tell you.

Just where was the actual purchase made? Boston, Las Vegas, Omaha, or at a point equidistant from all three? I am not sure, and neither is anyone else. What should you do in such a case? Many folks just go right ahead and make their good-faith effort to work things out. Then if they cannot solve the problem with the merchant, they notify the credit card company to stop payment. They ignore the 100-mile limitation when they make their complaint to the credit card company. They may be completely, legally correct in doing this.

Two courts that have dealt with this issue are in New York State. In the first case, *Lincoln Bank v. Carlson*,* Judge Kuszynski (a true friend of the credit card user), said: "To this court's mind, [judges often write like that] the statement that a card issuer is subject to all defenses if a transaction occurred less than 100 miles from the cardholder's address, *does not automatically presume a cardholder to give up all his defenses should the transaction take place at a distance of greater than 100 miles from the mailing address* [emphasis added]." In other words, the court said you have the right to use a good-faith stop within

---

*103 Misc. 2d 467 (1980), which means that the court opinion is found on page 467 in volume 103 of New York *Miscellaneous Reports, 2nd Series*, and that the case was decided in 1980. That information is for anyone who cares to go the county law library and look it up.

your billing address state or within 100 miles of your billing address. But, because the law explicitly gives you the right to stop payment within 100 miles or in the same state as your billing address, it does *not* mean you can't have those same rights more than 100 miles from your billing address.

In the other case on this issue, *Israelewitz v. Manufacturers Hanover Trust*, 465 New York Supplement, 2nd Series (New York City Civil Court, Small Claims Part, 1983), the judge, wrongly in my opinion, decided that the 100-mile, billing state requirements were legal.

So it is anybody's guess as to what the real rule is, and your guess is as good as the card companies'—maybe better.

But there *is* legal authority (good old Judge Kuszynski) for overriding the 100-mile, home-state limit on your good-faith stop-payment rights. There is also a recent case, *Hyland v. First USA Bank*, 2995 WL 595861 (Eastern District of PA), available on the WestLaw computer service (or by individual order from WestLaw at 800-562-2329 for about $12), which says that the card company's assurances and attempts at help to a card user victimized by an overseas merchant waives the 100-mile limit. Federal District Judge Giles said that when the bank says that it will help consumers resolve a problem, it can't come back later and say that the 100-mile limit applies and it won't help after all. Since credit card companies generally send out form letters saying they're going to look into your billing error complaint, the Hyland case may mean that the 100-mile limit is pretty much gone. That remains to be seen, but maybe there's actually something pro-consumer happening here!

Of course, nothing can stop you from just acting in good, lawful conscience as though that limitation doesn't exist. There are advantages to doing so, from the credit card user's point of view. For one, you are always in a better position to get your problems solved before you pay the bill. And, the credit card company may neither know nor care how far it is from Omaha, Nebraska, or wherever your billing address is to Boston, Massachusetts, or wherever you made your purchase. It might very well just charge back the disputed amount to the merchant and tell him to work things out with you himself. The distance issue might never come up. You will never know unless you try it. After all, I have spoken with many card company workers who do not know that this limitation on stop payments exists. (I have also spoken with many who do not know that the right to stop payment even exists!)

*A For-Sure Exception to the Limits.* The $50, 100-mile, or within your billing address state limits do not apply if you use a card issued by the company you are buying the wuzzy from or from a company affiliated with the card issuing company. This means if you buy a non-wuzzing wuzzy from, say Sears in Boston, for $11.97, using your Sears charge card, and your billing address is in Washington, D.C., you can do a good-faith stop.

Or if the card company sends you the offer, even if it is made by another company, the limits do not apply. Suppose you get, with your card bill, an offer for an eleven-piece cookware set at $29.95. You order the set. The frying pan melts like butter when you put it on the stove. The cookware company refuses to make good. You can certainly make a good-faith stop on the $29.95, even though it is less than $50, because the card company was involved in sending out the solicitation.

### Mail and Phone Orders

Another point about the 100-mile/home state limits on stop payments applies to things you buy by mail or over the telephone. Where is a sale by a merchant you call up on an 800, toll-free number really made? In effect, the merchant is in your hometown. He is looking for business nationwide by giving out a number you can call for free from anywhere in the country.

Even if you do not use an 800 number and pay for the call yourself, the merchant might legally be making the sale at the place you call from. A strong trend in American law today says that when a merchant goes after business in another state he is really in or doing business in that state.

This goes for ordering by mail as well as for ordering by phone. Something you buy from a faraway merchant was probably legally bought at the spot where you mailed in, or called in, the order. The leading text on contract law, *Williston on Contracts*, says "acceptance [of an offer to sell something] is effective when it enters . . . [the method] of communication." This means if you buy something over the phone, the place of purchase is where you say into the receiver, "Okay, I'll take it." And that certainly makes it within 100 miles of your billing address, when you are ordering from home. The same rule applies when you mail a stamped letter. The place of purchase is where you mail the letter.

So if the wuzzy that won't wuz was ordered by mail or phone (or on the Internet), you can make a good case for doing a good-faith stop even if you are in a different state or more than 100 miles from the wuzzy vendor.

The Federal Reserve Board, which is supposed to interpret consumer credit law for us, has completely ducked this issue. There are no rules written down in law books that deal specifically with this issue, although a few cases have discussed it, for example *In re Standard Financial Management Corp.*, 94 Bankruptcy Rep. 213, a 1988 case in Massachusetts where place of sale of a telephone sale of coins was found to be the consumer's home.

---

The Federal Trade Commission put out its 1994 Mail & Telephone Order Rule (16 Code of Federal Regulations, Part 435), which cut out a loophole some merchants were using to take more than the thirty days the FTC allows for shipping of mail- or phone-ordered items. It used to be that a merchant could get all the information it needed to complete your order and then, by not actually charging your account until it was ready to ship (maybe the item you ordered was out of stock or never stocked until someone ordered it) could have an extra month or two beyond what should be the legal thirty-day limit after getting the order to ship. Now the FTC says to merchants: "The 'clock' on your obligation to ship or take other action under the Rule begins as soon as you receive a 'properly completed' order. An order is properly completed when you receive the correct full or partial (in whatever form you accept) payment, accompanied by all the information you need to fill the order. Payment may be by cash, check, money order, the customer's authorization to charge an existing account. . . . It is irrelevant when you post or deposit payment, when checks clear, or when your bank credits your account. **The clock begins to run when you receive a properly completed order.**" Interestingly, the Direct Marketing Association, the mail-order merchants' group, vigorously opposed this consumer protection change to the law.

---

Interestingly, the Internet is causing a lot of judicial thought about issues like this. A new California Court of Appeal decision (*Hall v. LaRonde* (1997) 56 Cal.App.4th 1342, 66 Cal.Rptr.2d 399) held that Hall (in California) and LaRonde (in New York) had a continuing relationship over the Internet, where LaRonde sold Hall some software.

This meant that Hall could sue LaRonde in California courts and force LaRonde to come out to the West Coast to defend the case. Some might argue that a telephone purchase paid for with a credit card initiates pretty much the same sort of relationship that made LaRonde come out to California and puts the place of purchase where the card user's telephone is located—i.e., your living room. This may mean that for telephone or mail credit card purchases there may well not be any 100-mile limit.

So, make your guess in your favor and assume the good-faith stop rules apply to your problem until convinced otherwise. And make sure you're mighty hard to convince.

Also, credit card companies generally have operating regulations (not part of the law but at least as important as the law to credit card operators) that require merchants who take telephone orders to credit all charge-backs (money the card company takes back from the merchant) for orders where the merchant does not have an imprinted, signed charge slip. This is something the merchant cannot possibly have when he takes an order over the phone. If you question a telephone order on your card bill you must be given credit for it. So if you have a problem with an over-the-phone purchase, the card companies' operating regulations give you an extra weapon. (But the card companies do not want you to know about that weapon. When was the last time a credit card company sent you a copy of its operating regulations? It would be a good thing if those operating regulations, at least the parts dealing with customer's rights, were made readily available to the public. Why not, for example, on the Internet?)

### Mail-order Credit Card Rights

Your stop-payment and billing error rights can have all sorts of interesting effects, many of them good for consumers; some of them not so good. Consider the tale, reported by Roberta Furger in the excellent "Consumer Watch" column of *PC World*. Furger tells the story of Richard Whitsitt, a CPA in Panama City, Florida. Mr. Whitsitt sent a check to a mail-order computer sales company in Michigan for a shiny new state-of-the-art model. The check was cashed, but he never got his computer. He tried diligently to get his money refunded, but no luck. Going to Michigan for legal action was not a reasonable solution. So resourceful Mr. Whitsitt ordered a second, identical system and charged it to his credit card. When the computer came, he asked the card company to charge back the payment, showing that he had already paid for an identical system by check. The charge back was made and CPA Whitsitt had his new, working computer, which he no doubt thinks is much better than a lawsuit in Michigan.

Now that's what I call serious pro-consumer karate. And it emphasizes an important point: the credit card is the mail and telephone buyer's best friend. If you order something by mail and it never comes, and you paid by check, you just might be out of luck. If you paid with a credit card you can exercise your billing error rights and avoid paying for something you never got. Credit cards are the *only* way to go for any kind of mail-order or phone purchase. In fact, credit cards in many ways created the giant new mail-order business in computers, software, and other goodies. Just pick up a copy of *Computer Shopper* and page through it to see thousands of ads for hundreds of thousands of high-tech products. Without the security that the credit card gives consumers in mail-order purchases, I wonder if mail-order computer buying would have ever gotten off the ground.

Of course, clever credit card mail-order ploys are not limited to the consumer. The Federal Trade Commission brought an action against Creditcard Travel Services for, among other naughty things, sending customers a notice that it had issued a credit to consumer's credit cards when it had not: "The defendants specifically told consumers in that notice not to contact their credit card company about the charge, and to allow 30–90 days for the credit to appear. The Fair Credit Billing Act, which would entitle these consumers to dispute the validity of credit card charges with the issuers of their credit cards, requires that consumers report billing errors within 60 days after the statement containing the charge was mailed." Thus, the company apparently wanted to stall any billing error queries by the cardholder until after the sixty-day period had expired, which could let it keep the money it said it had refunded.

There are many variations on this scam, all of which depend on getting the card user to wait until the sixty days for notice to the card company of billing error has run out. Obviously it pays to be aware of your mail-order credit card error correction rights and exercise them promptly, no matter what a merchant such as Creditcard Travel Services may tell you.

## Ultimate Responsibility

The credit card company, not the merchant, is ultimately responsible for seeing that your good-faith stop-payment rights are protected. The managements of credit card companies are (or should be) very worried about problems with stop payments. The card company's liability for messing up on a stop payment can be tremendous. Thousands and thousands of dollars. The company does not want to deal with this. There is no profit in it. So its reaction when it gets a complaint is mostly just to kick the problem back to the seller for resolution. The card companies call this charging back.

In a charge-back the card company plucks the money it earlier put into the merchant's bank account right out again and tells the merchant to solve the problem. If you eventually get your problem solved and tell the card company so, the company gives the seller back the money. If you do not get your problem solved, the company does not charge your account for the problem sum, and the merchant gets nothing.

From the card companies' point of view, this is the intelligent thing to do. Why fight with the card user when they can let the user and merchant fight instead? And at little cost to the card company.

Here is part of a sample contract between a merchant and a bank. It reveals how card companies want merchants to deal with cardholder complaints.

CARDHOLDER COMPLAINTS. Merchant acknowledges that under applicable law, it and Bank may be subject to claims and defenses arising out of any transaction in which a Card is used as a method of payment or to obtain an extension of credit. The amount of liability in connection with any such claim or defense may be fixed by applicable law as of a specific point in time. Accordingly, Merchant agrees that it will maintain in writing, with respect to each claim or defense asserted by a Cardholder involving a Credit sale or which the Total Sale Price exceeded $50 (exclusive of finance charges, late charges, etc.) of which Merchant receives notice, (a) the Cardholder's name, (b) the Account Number, (c) the date and time the Cardholder asserted his claim or defense to Merchant, (d) the nature of the claim or defense, and (e) the action which the Merchant took in an attempt to resolve the dispute. The Merchant shall furnish Bank with such information upon request. Merchant agrees to indemnify Bank for any liability (including all legal fees and costs) which Bank incurs as a result of Merchant's failure to comply with this provision.

This clause is meant to force the merchant to bear all the responsibility and costs of dealing with any cardholder complaint for any purchase over $50. For example, the clause says that the merchant must keep a written record of all complaints on such purchases. It is probably *impossible* for a merchant to do this. If you come into a store and tell a salesclerk that you are unhappy with your new stereo, what do you think are the chances of his knowing about or writing up the complex notice of the dispute that the above clause requires? The clerk already has more than enough to do.

What this clause is really about is getting the bank off the hook and putting the merchant on the hook for any problems you have with the things you buy with a credit card. If the company charges back problem items to the merchant, it is off the hook.

By getting you, the customer, and the merchant involved in a fight, the card company avoids ultimate responsibility when you do a good-faith stop. Even so, the credit card company is still ultimately responsible for seeing that your order to stop payment is carried out.

What if the card company can't get back the money it paid out to the merchant? Maybe he's disappeared or gone bankrupt. You *still* get your money back. Suppose you have a new $999 garage door installed by DoorBuster, which has its office a mile from your house. A couple of weeks after installation you push the remote opener button and the entire installation self-destructs. When you call DoorBuster their phone is disconnected, and when you go to the office a sign on the door says the company is out of business.

So you tell the credit card company that you are not satisfied with the goods and services you got. You have tried in good faith to resolve the problem with the seller and have been unable to do so. How can you work out a problem with a company that no longer exists? So you want the bill taken off your account.

You are exercising your right to make a good-faith stop payment. You do this before you have paid any part of the bill on which the DoorBuster's charge first shows up. But the credit card company says, "Sorry, we paid DoorBuster the money it billed your account for last month, when the bill came in, and DoorBuster took the money, closed its account and disappeared. Since we cannot get the money back from DoorBuster, you will have to pay us the $999. You cannot use the good-faith stop on this purchase."

The credit card company is lying to you. It does not matter if it cannot get the money back, no matter what the reason. *You have an absolute right to stop payment if the good-faith stop conditions are met*, as they are in this DoorBuster example.

The credit card company, even if it has already paid the seller, as it usually will have done by the time you get your statement, still has to honor your demand to stop payment. Since this will cost the credit card company money, it does not want to do this.

Insist on your stop-payment rights, and if you do not get those rights, complain to the credit card cops or (if you must) get a lawyer.

### The $50 Limit

Suppose you buy two video tapes at $26 each. You put both on the same charge slip for a $52 total. One is defective. Can you make a good-faith stop on the $52? Or have you lost your right to make a good-faith stop because, while the total purchase was over $50, the defective tape cost less than $50?

The law does not deal with this issue. Given the lack of clarity in the law, you may as well adopt the position, which best protects you—the consumer, that any purchase that totals over $50 is covered by the good-faith stop clause of the law. Frankly, I doubt the billing department of most credit card companies would be enough on the ball to ever raise this issue. Unless they are really dumb, they just charge the disputed amount back to the seller anyway, since that costs them much less than fighting with you over the whole thing.

### Avoiding Problems with the Partial Payments Rule

What if you make just a partial payment on your credit card account? Suppose you pay $100 of a $200 total on your monthly statement? And you later dispute a $120 charge on your account *after* you paid the $100?

Here are the rules the credit card company is supposed to follow in applying the payment for the purpose of figuring out if you have paid for a purchase you have complained about. Payment goes first to any late charges on your account, with the oldest late charges being paid off first. Then your money goes to pay off finance (interest) charges, again, with the oldest being paid off first. Next, your payment is applied to any other charges on the account. Again, the oldest are paid off first.

What happens if two or more charges are billed to your account on the same day is not clear from the Fed's regulations. If you have charged two or more items on the same charge slip, payment would, according to the Fed, be applied to each individual charged item in the same proportion the dollar amount of the unsatisfactory purchase bears to the total amount charged on the slip. For example, you go out to dinner with a pal and charge the tab for the $120 meal (you old sport, you). Your meal was okay. Your pal gets food poisoning from the steak tartare. You pay your entire bill when it comes in from the credit card company except for $60 to cover the cost of the meal that poisoned your pal. *Then* you complain to the restaurant. (That was a mistake! Don't wait to scream!)

Here's where the problem with the rules comes in. You can refuse to pay only $30 of the $60 that the poisoned meal cost. Under the Fed rules, the $60 you paid wasn't applied to the good meal, as you might reasonably expect. Instead, $30 was applied to your meal and $30 to the poisoned meal.

This is pretty silly. The Federal Reserve Board could have adopted a rule that would have applied all your $60 payment to the good meal and none of it to the bad meal. The credit card companies think that the Fed's present rule is better for them, though, and that may just be the reason it was adopted.

Fortunately, if you follow this book's advice you will not have any problem with this. Complain to the seller or the credit card company *before* you pay anything on your account. Then you are protected from this foolish application of the Federal Reserve Bank Board's rules.

*Complain about the entire amount you charged.* In the poisoned meal example just above, when you complain about the meal be sure to place the entire $120 under the stop-payment order. Otherwise, your desire to be fair and pay that part of the bill that covers the okay, un-poisoned meal may lead you into the same pitfall of being able to stop payment on only $30 of the $60 price of the bad meal.

### Things to Remember About the Good-Faith Stop

If you need to do a good-faith stop payment, keep the following summary of the requirements discussed above in mind:

1. It can be used only for purchases totaling $50 or more.
2. The purchase must have been within 100 miles of the billing address, or in the same state as billing address (with possible exceptions discussed on pages 113–18).

3. You must make a good-faith effort to resolve the problem with the seller (this effort can be by oral notice).
4. You can stop payment only on unpaid amounts. That is, your oral or written complaint to either the credit card company or the merchant freezes the amount you can stop payment on.
5. Once you have complained to credit card company or merchant, even if you thereafter pay the disputed bill in part or in full, you ought to get your money back.
6. There is no special written form for complaint. A spoken complaint to merchant or bank is just as good as a written one.
7. Exceptions 1 and 2 above (the $50 and 100-mile limits) do not apply if the card was issued by the seller or an affiliated company, or if the card company solicited, by mail or some other way, your purchase.

## The Sixty-Day Stop

In the previous section we talked about the good-faith stop. But what if you don't meet the requirements for the good-faith stop? Suppose you spent less than $50 on something that does not work or that you bought more than 100 miles from your billing address and outside your home state. Then the good-faith stop does not apply. How can you get your money back?

Use the sixty-day stop. I call it the sixty-day stop because you must take action within sixty days of the time the credit card company sends you the statement that shows the charge for the whatever you want to stop payment on. The sixty-day stop-payment law gives you the right not to pay for goods or services you didn't get (as is only fair), and for goods and services that are not delivered to you as you agreed.

Within that sixty days—which starts running the day the company *mails* the statement to you, *not* when you *get* the statement—you must notify the company *in writing* that you are refusing to pay for the billed goods or services because they were not accepted by you or were not delivered to you as agreed.

According to the Federal Reserve Board, here are some examples of what the sixty-day stop covers.

1. A charge on your monthly statement for a charge where you refused the goods because they were not what you had ordered.
2. Delivery to you of goods or services different from those which you ordered or agreed upon with the seller.
3. Delivery to you of the wrong amount.
4. Late delivery.
5. Delivery to the wrong location.

The Fed also says, in that obscure dialect called "we don't want to take the responsibility," that the sixty-day "stop does not apply to a dispute relating to the quality of property or services that a consumer accepts. Whether acceptance occurred is determined by state or other applicable law." My interpretation: You can use a sixty-day stop if you do not get what you agreed on with the seller when you made the purchase.

### Acceptance—What Is It?

Time to explain a little legal jargon. You can use the sixty-day stop if you did not accept the stuff you ordered. That is what the Federal Reserve Board's rules say.

What the Fed does not say is that "acceptance" is what lawyers call a term of the art. In the legal world, a term of the art is a word that does not mean what most people think it does. Acceptance does *not* mean that you took the stuff when the seller gave it to you. It means that it met all the requirements of your deal with the seller. That is, if you take something you bought, use it, and are totally satisfied with it, and that there are no hidden problems with it that come out later, then you have accepted it.

Suppose you buy a squirt gun at the dimestore. You get home, fill the red plastic machine gun with water, and try to blast Fido. The gun won't squirt.

The squirt gun did not meet all the requirements of our deal with the dimestore, such as the unspoken but real desire for a gun that squirts. Legally, you probably have not accepted the gun. Had you used your Visa card to pay for the gun, you could refuse to pay for the unsquirting squirter when it showed up on your monthly Visa statement, even if the charge was only $1.19.

A reasonable interpretation of this section of the Truth in Lending Act would allow you to use the sixty-day stop on any purchase at all if the purchase did not do what it was supposed to do.

Law Professor Ralph J. Rohner says in his excellent book, *The Law of Truth in Lending*:

> [The Fed] . . . lists as a billing error "delivery of property or services different from that agreed upon." This could equally refer to goods of the wrong size or color, or goods of defective construction that did not satisfy the implied warranty of merchantability [a warranty of merchantability means you can use the stuff for what you bought it for].
>
> Similarly, it is not altogether clear whether there is a billing error when a consumer revokes acceptance of goods previously delivered. . . . Technically, these goods are not "accepted."

Professor Rohner also says about the sixty-day stop, "The line between defective quality and improper delivery can be very faint." To translate, I think Rohner is saying that there is not much, if any, difference between not accepting something and buying something that does not satisfy you. And the law says that if you do not accept something, you can stop payment on the charge.

Card companies tend to really *hate* this provision of the law. It gives you very powerful stop-payment rights. The companies do not want you stopping payment, because they think it is bad for profits. They will argue vehemently that this provision of the law does not give you stop-payment rights. They are wrong. But they keep on arguing because they do not want to believe that you have this right. Be ready for a fight when you use this stop-payment provision of the law.

Merchants aren't too wild about this provision of the law either. In fact, a lot of them have adopted a rather sneaky phrasing on the charge slip you are asked to sign when it's printed out on the point-of-sale terminal. There is a little statement above the space for your signature that says something like: "I agree that the goods or services paid for with this charge have been delivered and that I have accepted those goods or services."

There is no sensible reason for this statement, because no matter what the slip says and no matter what you sign when the slip is thrust into your face with twenty-three other folks in line behind you, the consumer protection laws that regulate credit card transactions still control.

This is what is sometimes called a terror clause. The merchant or the card company want to wave this slip with its signed statement at you later on if you seek to assert your sixty-day stop-payment rights. You are supposed to believe that by signing the slip with the terror clause you have somehow waived your consumer protection rights. Not so.

### Differences Between the Good-Faith and Sixty-Day Stops

To sum up: There is not a big difference between the sixty-day-stop and the good-faith stop when it comes to what they cover. The difference is more in how you execute them.

While these two laws/rights are not that different, the special circumstances of your situation might make one preferable to the other. The important point is that you can assert them both (even at the same time) to protect yourself. If you assert both rights at once, there is no chance you will not have used the right one.

Generally, you should place more emphasis on the good-faith stop because this interpretation of the sixty-day stop may be (to say the least) unfamiliar to most credit card company workers. That does not mean it is out of line or wrong, only that they do not know about it. The average credit card company employee—and the above average too, for that matter—has little or no interest in understanding the complexities of *your* credit card rights. As far as I know, no card companies hand out bonuses to employees who take interest in the rights of customers.

### The Sixty-Day Stop-Payment Process

In the case of the sixty-day stop the credit card company is required by law to do the following: Within thirty days after getting your letter it must respond in writing, acknowledging your notice. The company does not have to make any final decision about your stop payment in those thirty days. It only has to write to tell you that it has your notice.

The only exception to this required thirty-day response by the company to your stop-payment demand is *if* the company can solve the problem you complain about before the thirty days are up. Then your next statement should show a credit that corrects the problem. That is, it must show a credit for the payment you want to stop.

If the company does not credit your account within thirty days, then your next bill must include a notice that you need not pay any disputed amounts. Some card companies print this notice on every statement so

## DIFFERENCES BETWEEN THE GOOD FAITH
## AND SIXTY-DAY STOPS

| | Good-faith-stop | Sixty-day-stop |
|---|---|---|
| **Geographic** | Mostly good only in your billing address state or within 100 miles of your billing address and for purchases over $50. Limits don't apply to purchases from card issuer or affiliates. | Good throughout the world. |
| **Procedure** | Notice can be oral or written; can be made to either merchant or card company. Card holder must attempt to resolve problem with merchant before stopping. | Notice must be in writing to card company at special address. |
| **Penalties** | No automatic up-to-$50 penalty. | Automatic— amount of disputed charge up to $50. |
| **Law suit rights** | For both good-faith and sixty-day stops you can sue a card company if it does not follow the rules and collect statutory damages, attorney's fees and actual damages if you win. | |
| **Time good for** | Unlimited time, if merchant or bank notified of dispute before bill paid. | Only sixty days after day statement showing disputed charge is mailed to card holder. |

that they do not have to worry about violating this requirement. Some put it on the back of the statement in tiny little print.

The card company does not have to put on the bill the amount you need not pay and does not have to deduct it from the total owed it puts on the bill.

Then within ninety days or two billing periods, whichever is shorter, of the time it first got your notice, the card company *must:*

1. correct the error you complained about—in the case of a sixty-day stop this would mean taking the complained-of amount permanently off your bill—and notify you that this has been done.

or

2. send you a written explanation, after conducting a reasonable investigation, why it thinks the bill was correct, and, if you ask, also send you copies of the charge slips.

or

3. correct any error it does find (even if it's not the one you complained about).

While it is investigating the problem you wrote about, the card company must include a notice on the bills that it sends you saying something along the lines of "You need not pay any disputed amount." This notice can be printed on every bill, even if nothing is in dispute on the account—that's the way most companies do it.

Just how much time does the card company have to resolve your billing error complaint? Two full billing periods *after* the card company gets your written billing error notice, or ninety days at most if the billing cycle is, say, quarterly, rather than monthly. So if you mail the billing error letter on June 10, the card company gets the letter on June 13 and your billing cycle (the cutoff date for billing, *not* the date the bill is mailed) started on June 1 and the first of every month, the card company has until September 1 to investigate and send you its final resolution.

That doesn't mean its final letter to you can be postmarked September 2. Of course, you'll know the date the company got the letter because the return receipt you requested will come back to you with that date entered on it by the post office. Or you'll have enclosed a check with the letter and the deposit date on the back of that check will tell you the latest day the letter enclosed with the check could have been received.

This time limit is a very important protection for you. Many card companies either can't or won't obey the time limits, and like to come back to you many months after the ninety-day maximum billing error resolution has expired with a letter claiming that they have now completed their investigation and are deleting their temporary credit of the disputed amount and are recharging your account. But sadly (for the card companies), this is illegal. And rightly so. Consumers shouldn't have to wait for a year to have a billing error problem resolved.

Remember, you have very powerful stop-payment rights to exercise in a proper case. And it shouldn't cost you anything, unlike stopping a check.

### No Charge to Stop Payment on Your Card

If you stop payment on a check, the bank can charge you up to $35, even though it costs a bank hardly anything to handle a stop-payment order. The big fee discourages you from stopping payment. If you do stop payment on a check, the bank profits.

When you stop payment with a credit card, the card company is forbidden by law to charge you anything. That's right; federal law does not allow card companies to charge you anything when you exercise your credit card stop-payment rights. So stopping payment on a credit card bill is a lot more attractive than stopping payment on a check.

It may not make a lot of sense to stop payment on a $50 check if the bank charges $35 for the dubious privilege. It may make lots of sense to stop payment on a $50 charge when the card company must do the stop for free.

On page 131 is a sample letter disputing a card company's attempt to rebill a disputed charge after the ninety-day period.

While the card company is investigating your written report, it can't try to collect any disputed amount and can't report that you aren't paying what you owe to any credit bureaus. It can't even *threaten* to report you to any credit bureaus.

However, it *can* try to collect any amounts you did not question. And it can report you delinquent on your account to credit bureaus if you do not pay the unquestioned amounts.

The company can and almost always will ask you for more information about your complaint. It can also ask the merchant to verify the sale. Then the company decides if your complaint is justified. Did you get what you ordered? Did it work? Did you accept it? Unfortunately, some companies almost always decide that the merchant is right and the card user is wrong. Some don't even bother to do any real investigation.

In any case, with the sixty-day stop, the company can apply the dis-

123 Nice Street
Finetown, Calif. 99999
June 24, 2001

Barbara Banker
Very Big Bank Customer Service Division
Retail Credit Division
1 VeryBig Plaza
Plazedale, New York 66666

RE: Visa account #1234567890

Dear Ms. Banker:

I have your letter of June 20, 2001, which arrived here today.

VeryBig Bank's attempt to rebill this previously disputed, very stale charge from over eight months ago is in violation of the Truth in Lending Act and applicable California law. Please correct this unlawful rebill of the purported $83.69 from Blamo Rent-a-Car immediately and advise me in writing that this has been done.

Please note that I continue to dispute this purported charge from Blamo, that I do not owe it, and that I will not pay it.

Please do not contact me in any attempt to collect this charge.

Sincerely yours,
Sally Well Informed

Certified Mail No. P 333 444 555—Return Receipt Requested

---

puted amount against your credit limit. This can be a serious inconvenience if you are close to going over the limit, since it means you may not be able to charge any more on that account. If you pay your account off in full every month, this will probably not be a problem, since you are not likely close to the limit anyhow.

## Billing Error Rule Changes by the Fed: Good for the Card Companies, Bad for Card Users

Recently the Federal Reserve Board added a section to the mighty *Official Staff Commentary on Regulation Z* that either cleared up or muddied up what card companies are supposed to do when you dispute a charge, depending on who you talk to about it. I call the *Staff Commentary* mighty because Congress gave the Fed the power to change the credit card laws it passed by changing Regulation Z and the *Staff Commentary*. That's pretty powerful stuff: change the law without going through Congress or the president.

A little background: For many years card companies have been required to make a reasonable investigation of billing error claims on your credit card account. But this rule didn't apply to claims of fraudulent charges (or so the card companies claimed).

Before the Fed's recent change to Regulation Z, in my view, card companies were required to make a "reasonable investigation" of claims of fraudulent charges by the cardholder. This probably included going to the merchant and independently investigating what happened. Many card companies tried to get around this expensive requirement by demanding that the cardholder provide all sorts of notarized statements and documents, often documents they knew the cardholder didn't have. The whole idea was to demand documents the cardholder couldn't provide and then to say they couldn't help with the problem.

It reminds me of the bureaucrat of fifty or so whose card bill one month showed tickets for a dozen heavy-metal rock concert tickets and several limo rides to those concerts. This gentleman hadn't been to a rock concert in twenty-five years and the charges were fraudulent. But, when he contested the charges, the card company told him that he would have to provide a police report on the fraud before they would look into the problem (remember, now, it's their job to investigate, not yours). He went to the police and was told that they wouldn't take a report on this low-priority matter because there was nothing they would be able to do about it: "It's the bank's problem" he was told.

It was a catch-22. The bank (illegally) refused to investigate without the police report, and the police wouldn't take a report. But he was an important city official and he knew the police chief personally. He went over to the chief's office and explained things. The chief told him that the bank demanded the report because it thought he couldn't get one and they could ignore his complaint and collect the money from him. Although the typical card user couldn't get the report, Mr. Executive did, because he knew the right people.

Amazingly, even after he sent in a copy of the police report, the card company still refused to credit his account, claiming that the whole thing was somehow his fault. He finally hired a lawyer and got things straightened out (no thanks to the bank), and even got some money from the bank in settlement. But he still wonders: What happens if you have fraudulent heavy-metal concert ticket charges on your account and you aren't a good friend of the chief of police? I hope you don't have to find out.

Anyway, the Fed issued the following changes on what reasonable investigation the bank has to make when fraud is claimed by the cardholder with the spin that it was going to help card users.

The Fed's change added this to the *Staff Commentary*:

> SETTLEMENT OF DISPUTE. A card issuer may not consider a dispute settled and report an amount as delinquent or begin collection of the disputed amount until it has completed a reasonable investigation of the cardholder's claim. A reasonable investigation requires an independent assessment of the cardholder's claim based on information obtained from both the cardholder and the merchant, if possible. In conducting an investigation, the card issuer may request the cardholder's reasonable cooperation. The card issuer may not automatically consider a dispute settled if the cardholder fails or refused to comply with the particular request. However, if the card issuer otherwise has no means of obtaining information necessary to resolve the dispute, the lack of information necessary to resolve the dispute, the lack of information resulting from the cardholder's failure or refusal to comply with a particular request may lead the card issuer to reasonably terminate the investigation. (Section 226.12(c)(2))

This statement was touted by at least one consumer financial magazine as a change that would now require the card companies to conduct a reasonable investigation instead of just accepting whatever story the merchant cooks up. But before the change, the card company was still required to conduct a reasonable investigation. Given that, you might reasonably infer that the effect of adding the above clause might be to weaken the investigation that the card companies had to make when you dispute a charge.

*What Might Really Happen When You Ask for an Investigation?*
In fact, a card company may not be in a position to conduct a reasonable investigation of most problems—at least not at what it considers to be a reasonable price. Nonetheless, the card companies set up and control the card system, and they are certainly in the best position to investigate. They must be responsible for the system they created and run.

If you tell the card company you are not paying for the roach-

## SAMPLE ANTI-RUN-AROUND LETTER

123 Card User Avenue
FineTown, California 90000
December 39, 2020

President Rudolphia Green
RunAround Credit Card Company
345 Corporate RunAround Thruway
Bananas, South Dakota 57000

Dear President Green:

This letter is about my credit card account number 1234567890 with your company.

On September 23, I wrote to your billing error correction department at the address indicated on my statement about my desire to exercise my rights not to pay the charge for $88.65 that appeared on the July 1 statement from Roach Haven Hotel in Santa Barbara.

On October 22, I received a letter from your Mr. Bug stating that he needed to know exactly and precisely what species of roaches I had found objectionable during my stay. He enclosed a photocopy of a statement from Roach Haven Hotel stating: "No roaches have ever been found in our fine establishment, at least not so anyone can prove."

Mr. Bug's letter said "that a temporary credit for $88.65 has been applied to your account. We must hear from you within 10 (ten) days to maintain this credit on your account."

I responded with the requested information in a letter on November 2.

On November 25, I received a second letter from Mr. Bug dated November 11 and postmarked November 24 which demanded that I provide an exact count of the number of roaches that had spent the night with me in room 5678 at Roach Haven. And an estimate of the total weight of the roaches. And a copy of any Santa Barbara city or county ordinance that forbids roaches from inhabiting a hotel room with a human being. And pictures of all the roaches with a copy of their family trees for twenty-seven generations back. And also stating "that a temporary credit for $88.65 has been applied to your account. We must hear from you within 10 (ten) days to maintain this on your account."

President Green, I think I am getting the runaround. You do not need all this information. And if you did, it could have all been requested in your company's first letter to me.

Please see to it that a permanent credit is immediately made to my account before I am forced to consider filing a complaint with the appropriate agencies for RunAround's failure to comply with the Truth in Lending Act (15 U.S.C. 1601 et seq.).

Sincerely,
Mary Credit

Certified Mail # P 987-654-321—Return Receipt Requested

infested hotel room you stayed in in Santa Barbara, a reasonable investigation could involve sending someone to Santa Barbara to see if the room really is roach-infested. That could cost a lot more than the room. Writing to the hotel for a statement that the room is not roach heaven is most likely not a reasonable investigation.

Before the Fed's change in the rules, the Federal Trade Commission had in 1994 charged Dillard's Department Stores with violating the Truth in Lending Act by placing unreasonable burdens on cardholders trying to get unauthorized or fraudulent charges removed from their accounts. The FTC's complaint said that cardholders often couldn't get the unauthorized charges removed from their accounts unless they signed a notarized affidavit entitled "Declaration of Fraud Under Penalty of Perjury," provided copies of police reports, came into Dillard's stores to answer questions about the charges and agreed in writing to testify in court.

The FTC, after the Fed's rule changes, dropped its complaint against Dillard's. David Medine, associate director for credit practices at the FTC, said that the new Fed rule would have made the Dillard's case very tough to prove. The Fed, said Mr. Medine, by setting the legal standard too high, has made it very tough to bring future cases against card issuers. "If consumers start perceiving that they can't get unauthorized charges off their credit card bills, they're going to be very reluctant to carry credit cards around," Mr. Medine concludes.

Yet under the law the card company must reasonably investigate your complaint or credit your account. So the smart thing, from the company's point of view, is to credit your account and charge back the contested sum to Roach Haven Hotel. This lets it duck its legal responsibility for investigating your problem. Still, it does not want to upset the merchants by charging back lots of purchases. The company must make its decision with the knowledge that if it decides wrongly you can take it to court for a very expensive lawsuit.

Some companies appear to have decided that the best thing to do in this situation is to just ignore your letter. They figure they can always claim it got "lost." Others will respond to your letter with a statement that they need more information. When you write to them with the requested information, they still need "more information."

### Other Alternatives

What if you can't meet all the requirements for a sixty-day stop or good-faith stop? Maybe you didn't read this book until more than sixty days after you got the bill for an unsatisfactory purchase.

Does that mean you are completely out of luck? Happily, no. The card companies have operating regulations, which are the internal rules of Visa or MasterCard. These operating regulations, which are part of the contract between the card companies and the banks that actually issue the Visa or MasterCard, may give you additional rights over and above what the law gives you. You can complain to the Visa or MasterCard organizations if you are not happy with the card company's resolution of any problem. See the addresses in the Resources section.

---

#### • CREDIT CARD INSIDER'S TIP •

Be sure to send your written complaint letter of any sort to the special billing error address found on your monthly statement. It is almost certainly not the same as the address you send your check to. And remember, a telephone call, fax, or E-mail will probably not protect your billing error legal rights.

---

# Identity Theft and Your Privacy

Identity fraud is digging deep into consumers' pockets. The perpetrator may use a variety of tactics to drain your finances: posing as a loan officer and ordering your credit report (which lists account numbers); "shoulder surfing" at the ATM or phone booth to get your PIN code; "dumpster diving" in trash bins for unshredded credit applications, canceled checks or other bank records; or, until recently, notifying the Postal Service to redirect your mail to the address of choice, such as a mail drop, which allows anonymity. It may be months before you're aware you're a victim.

—Advisory issued by the Chief Postal Inspector

Identity theft may be the least known but fastest-growing crime in America. It is certainly a very profitable one. But what exactly is it?

The Ralph Nader–affiliated California Public Interest Research Group (CalPIRG) in its special report *Theft of Identity: The Consumer X-Files* says: "From changing your address to theirs to illegally obtaining your credit report, from reading your motor vehicle registration records to dumpster-diving for your employers' old files, identity thieves are fraudulently assuming thousands of consumers' identities a year and ruining lives." CalPIRG goes on to say: "'Theft of Identity' fraud occurs in a variety of ways and has many labels. In general, identity-thieves take pieces of your personal identifying information, such as your name, address, phone number, social security number, driver's license number, date of birth, credit and bank account numbers—any information you would use to verify your identity."

Two key variations on identity theft are referred to by law enforcement agencies as true-name frauds and account-takeover frauds. In true-name fraud, the crook uses your personal identification information to get new credit cards in your name. For example, using information obtained from a dishonest bank employee (or perhaps found in the bank's trash), the crook may know your address, phone number, social security number, and driver's license number as well as where you work. Once the new cards are in the crook's hands, he or she may apply for new loans in your name, rent an apartment in your name, or open utility accounts in your name. Reselling overseas calls for cash on a phone number in your name which the crook will never pay for is especially profitable, particularly when done from an apartment rented in your name on which the rent will never be paid.

In account-takeover fraud the crook gets some personal identification information about you to tap into already existing bank or credit accounts. For example, the crook can put in a change of address form with the post office to have your new credit cards or credit card statements sent to an address, such as a mail drop, controlled by the thief. Or the crook may just call up your bank, and with your identification information (such as your date of birth and social security number, easily, if illegally, gotten from a credit report) have another card on your already existing account sent to that mail-drop address.

Steve Shaw, a one-time victim of identity theft, now an expert in the subject, told U.S. PIRG: "TOI [theft of identity] eradicates any need to counterfeit money, checks, or credit cards. Why run the risk and go to the trouble of forging financial instruments when somebody else's personal information will trigger the issuance of *genuine* items? In the rush to extend credit, make additional sales, and profit from interest charges, creditors are more than willing to function, in effect, as counterfeiting service bureaus. And their counterfeit is the best in the world, indistinguishable from the real thing because it *is* the real thing."

How can you protect yourself against identity theft? Usually this sort of question is answered by the media with a list of two or three rather ineffectual things the consumer can try.

In fact, there isn't that much you, the cardholder, can do. The credit card system is fundamentally insecure and is wide open to fraud and identity theft. The system the card companies constructed wasn't set up to stop identity theft. It was set up to make card use very easy and to give the card companies big profits. Lack of security, the other side of the coin of simplicity, was not the biggest concern.

There used to be real protection in the fact that there were lots more folks with credit cards than there were identity thieves and the odds were more or less with you. Now the odds are dropping fast against the honest cardholder as more and more crooks find out just how easy and profitable identify theft is and how insecure the card system is.

Let's look at one composite, hypothetical case study of identity theft. Bill, age twenty-six, holds an MBA from the University of California at Berkeley's Haas School of Business and works out of his house as a consultant in an esoteric area of municipal finance. One day Bill got a call from Men's Super Suit Wonderhouse ("No Suit Over $5,000, Alterations Extra"), telling him he owed it $18,000-plus dollars because MSSW had opened an account for Bill's "son," who had said he had authorization to use Bill's social security number. Bill's only son is two years old and rarely shops for $5,000 suits. When Bill asked for the name of his so-called son, he recognized it as that of an accountant he'd had brief contact with through one of his clients, a guy who had access to Bill's social security number and other personal information in Bill's supplier file with the client.

Super Suit told Bill to check with the credit reporting agencies, get copies of his credit reports, and see if any other fraudulent accounts had been opened in his name. Super Suit said it would drop its purported claims against Bill after he sent it a notarized statement (at a notary fee of $10) saying he would file criminal charges against the crook.

Then Bill went to the Berkeley police to file charges against the crook. At first the police refused to take a report, and it was only after Bill contacted one of his Haas School classmates, now working in the mayor's office, that he was able to get the police to take a report. He says, "The cops told me that it was policy not to take reports on credit card fraud— they just don't have the manpower and they concentrate on violent crimes. If I hadn't used my connections, which I don't think the average guy has, I wouldn't have been able to make the report and Super Suit would probably still be after me for the fraudulent charges. In fact, one of the cops told me off the record that lots of card companies know that many police departments don't want to take reports on credit card fraud and that's why the companies demand you make a report. Then they tell you, 'You didn't get the report we told you to get, so pay up, you crook.'"

The case was transferred to the San Francisco police department (apparently because Super Suit was in San Francisco). The SFPD told Bill he had done everything he could, but if the crook tried to open another account, the store could decide to press charges. No one explained why the Super Suit account wasn't cause enough for criminal prosecution or why Super Suit wasn't pursuing the crook.

Then Bill got his credit reports! His Experian report was ten pages long with thirty-seven overdue phony accounts. And two court judgments against Bill (or at least in his name) for overdue rent and an eviction from a Palo Alto apartment Bill had never been to and for repossession of a Mercedes-Benz convertible Bill had never seen by Palo Alto Auto Leasing.

Bill went to the district attorney's office. There he was told there was nothing they could do because the eviction and the repossession were civil matters and he should write to the judges in each case. Bill did write, to no effect, and he was later told by a friendly clerk at the courthouse that the judge never looked at these cases, judgment was entered by the clerk with a rubber stamp, and the judge was too swamped to even think about doing something unless Bill hired a lawyer to make formal (and expensive) motions.

Bill next got Experian and the other credit reporting agencies to put a fraud statement on his credit report so that, theoretically, he would be notified before any new credit applications in his name were approved. (This is useful, but far from infallible, much like the credit reporting system.) But Experian then demanded that Bill contact each of the thirty-seven fraudulent creditors and send each and every one of them one of those $10 notarized statements to prove that a criminal report was filed—$370 down the tubes.

Bill got a notice from Wonderful Leasing of the SouthEast Bay that he had defaulted on his new, custom convertible Lexus's lease (Bill is still driving the Chevy Blazer he bought while in graduate school). And National Collections started calling him demanding that he pay for his Lexus lease. Bill sent in a notarized $10 statement to SouthEast Bay, but the calls keep on coming.

Next, Bill was rear-ended by a guy with no insurance. The police came to take a report and arrested Bill! It turned out that one of the merchants the crook had defrauded had sworn out a warrant against the crook and against Bill, too! And Bill's name was listed in the Automated Criminal History System. So he got busted, even though he was completely innocent of any wrongdoing. After his wife bailed him out, he was able, after hiring a lawyer, to get the charges dropped. The lawyer says Bill may have a good case for damages against the merchant that swore out the warrant, to which Bill says, "Great, just what I need, more headaches."

Bill estimates that he has spent over 120 hours of his time trying to resolve the theft of his identity and is very stressed out over the whole thing. He says, "I'm afraid to answer the phone these days. It's probably going to be another collection call on an account I never opened and don't know anything about. I'm afraid of being arrested again for no good reason."

Bill thinks that the only reason that he has been able to make any progress at all is because he is sophisticated and experienced in business matters and because he works at home, can make numerous personal phone calls during business hours, and can use his secretary and his computer and laser printer to write letters. He did manage to at least temporarily get his name off the computerized police list of folks who should get arrested.

He thinks the average non-MBA would not be able to make the police reports the creditors demand because the police just wouldn't take them; in fact, Joe Plain Citizen just plain wouldn't be able to figure out what to do. For that matter, *Bill's* not so sure he has figured out what to do. His credit is still messed up, he's had to put off moving to a bigger house because the mortgage company had doubts about his explanation of the fraudulent defaults on his credit reports, and the collection calls keep on coming.

Bill says: "I did nothing wrong. I am the victim, pure and simple. My credit is a mess. Now Wonderful Leasing is calling me and says they are going to sue me and have the cops put me in jail. What a system!"

So how do you protect yourself so you don't end up like Bill? There are a few steps you can take, but what's truly needed is drastic reform of the credit reporting system. One thing you could do to move this forward would be to join and work with one of the many state Public Interest Research Groups (for more information, see the resources under Consumer Groups).

This is not a situation where you are doing something wrong and can solve the problem by making a few simple changes. Unfortunately, and frighteningly, the credit system (and you) are horribly vulnerable to identity theft and fraud. Indeed, the *more* responsible and honest you are, the *bigger* your chances of being an identity theft victim.

Consumer attorney and crusader against identity theft David Szwak of Shreveport, Louisiana, told me at a lawyers conference that "identity thieves like to target those who have perfect credit and payment histories." And why not? If a crook is going to steal someone's credit identity, it might as well be a really good one that can be used to rack up some really big bills.

Until the card companies and credit bureaus come up with some decent security for the system, there can be no guarantee that you won't be victimized by this infuriating crime (and probably even more infuriated by the complete lack of help you'll get from your card company and the credit bureaus). Indeed, Experian admitted that it opened a computer hot-line access account to its credit files for a Long Beach, California, mortgage company and sold the company plenty of reports. Then Experian discovered the "mortgage company" was run by a fraud ring from Nigeria looking for really good candidates for identity theft. Then there's the case of Autoland, a car dealer in Springfield, New Jersey, that found out its employees were selling crooks credit files gotten over Autoland's credit reporting terminals.

As Texas Attorney General Dan Morales writes in his *Consumer Watch Newsletter*: "It is often impossible to know if your financial identity has been stolen until long after the fact. The first clues may come from a bill collector calling about an overdue shopping account at a store halfway across the country, a telephone bill containing long-distance calls you never made, or an application for a mortgage denied due to a bad credit report." In other words, the crook steals your credit identity, makes off with thousands of dollars in items charged to you, messes up your credit, and you don't even find out about it until months or years later. It's getting close to the perfect crime, from the crook's point of view, especially the part when the victim doesn't find out until long, long after the theft.

Now let's talk about the simple but not terribly effective things you can do to protect yourself against identity theft, and then we'll get into the not-so-simple, but very powerful secret weapon you can wield against card companies that let your identity be stolen.

## Simple Things to Do Against Identity Theft

**1.** Minimize the contents of your wallet or purse. Carry only a few credit cards and nothing with your social security number on it (this may be a little tough to do in those states that foolishly use your social security number as your driver's license number).

2. Be sure your mailbox at home is securely locked or use a post office box.

3. Have your name and address removed from the phone book.

4. Take a look at your credit reports from Experian (formerly TRW), TransUnion, and Equifax every year or so. The charge should be around $8 each unless you live in one of the advanced states that require the credit reporting agencies to provide free copies to consumers. If you see some accounts you know nothing about, you may be a victim.

5. Have the credit bureaus note in your file that no account is to be opened unless the credit grantor calls you at a specified number and gets your okay. This is best done by certified mail, return receipt requested, to each credit bureau, even if you make the initial contact with a bureau by phone.

6. Tell the credit bureaus that you do not want your file accessed for prescreened credit offers. Those "You have already been approved" junk-mail offers you get come from "prescreening" of credit reports. The card company tells the credit bureau it wants a list of, say, all folks in Zip Code 11111 who make over $40,000 a year and haven't gone bankrupt in the last three months and who have more than two kids. Then the solicitations are sent out (to the joy of identity thieves who know how easy it is to steal one of those solicitations, change the address to a mail drop rented by the thief, send it in, and get some very useful plastic in the mail).

Some states, such as California, require the bureaus to do this on request. But there's no harm in asking in any state. Of course, then you will no longer get those preapproved applications for credit cards you don't need (seventeen a year for every adult in America) in the mail.

7. Have very few open credit card accounts. Keep track of when the bills for each account you use are supposed to come in. Stealing account statements from the mail or mailboxes and using the information inside to tell the card company to change the address to a crook-controlled address is a common method of seizing one or more of your credit accounts. If you don't notice that you haven't gotten a bill, you won't have any way to quickly find out you are a victim.

8. Be *very* cautious (indeed, downright obnoxious) about refusing to give out your social security number, driver's license number, mother's maiden name, or other personal identification information. This information can be the key to your credit files for an identity thief.

9. Ask the credit bureaus to take your credit information off-line. Almost all credit reports can be accessed by any subscriber to the system. And there are millions of subscribers at used car lots, banks, credit unions, and retailers. But when a report is off-line it can't be accessed without your okay. This is done all the time for celebrities and politicians including, reportedly, Bill Clinton and O.J. Simpson. VIP information is kept in a special manual-access-only file. The bureaus are less than eager to do this for the average person because it means that the manual file can't be accessed by the profitable (for the bureaus) computer method, but only by written request with the credit report going out in the mail, which is much more costly for the bureau.

Okay, so you've done all the right stuff, and you're *still* a victim of the insecure credit system, a victim of identity theft. What to do?

Your only realistic option may be to unholster a lawsuit. But remember, a lawsuit should be your last resort. You may have to get a lawyer and start suing under a little-used section of the federal Truth in Lending Act (15 U.S.C. 1642). That section makes it illegal to issue a credit card in anyone's name without that person's explicit permission. If you are the victim of identity theft and have a fraudulent credit card account opened in your name, you certainly did not apply for the account and the law has been broken.

This law was passed in the seventies when card companies were throwing unrequested and unapplied-for cards into the mail to just about everybody in America (including reportedly many dogs and cats). The resulting wave of unreported stolen cards (folks couldn't report the nonarrival of a card they didn't know was coming) and fraud led Congress to forbid the issuing of a credit card to anyone who didn't ask for it.

That law applies just as well to a card company or retailer who opens an account in your name, based on a fraudulent application. A card company that opens a credit card account based on a fraudulent application also opens itself up to a lawsuit, with the losing card company paying your lawyer's fees.

A good way to understand this little-used, almost-secret section of the Truth in Lending Act is a little story. The names and details have been changed to protect the innocent and the guilty alike.

Roberta was a reporter on a great metropolitan newspaper. One day her 1968 Toyota Corolla blew its head gasket and she wandered by the local Ford dealer to look at a new Escort (they don't pay those reporters anything!). Roberta found one she liked and went in the back office to work out financing with the lady the salesman referred to as "Dr. Credit." Roberta smiled at the doctor and told her: "I have perfect credit. What's the lowest interest rate you've got?"

Unfortunately, the doctor, after a computerized check of Roberta's credit report, was unable to agree. She told Roberta that the report showed credit card accounts unpaid for over three months at Neiman-BloomingFields, Overpriced Furniture, and several other local retailers and also showed that Roberta had recently moved to an address in a rather seamy section of town called Dumpoville.

Roberta protested that she had never had accounts at any of those stores and hadn't moved away from the chic little street in HighHat-Town she loved so well. Dr. Credit was unmoved by the protests. "We go by what's on the screen," she was told. "But we'd be happy to take cash for the Escort." Roberta had to wait to get that new Ford.

When she looked into the fraudulent accounts she found that all the applications showed the Dumpoville address and all the statements were being mailed there. So she had no way to know that the accounts were even open without getting her credit report.

That is, she had no way until, right after the fiasco at the Ford dealer, the collection calls started coming in to her at home and at work. Roberta contacted all the creditors on the fraud accounts and explained what had happened. The response at Neiman-BloomingFields was typical: "Pay your bills, you deadbeat!" Now Roberta might have been happy to pay for the $18,000 ermine coat, if only she had at least had a chance to wear it. But Neiman-BloomingFields had delivered it to the Dumpoville address she'd never been to, or so they said. All the retailers and card companies wanted their money from Roberta. They were exceedingly uninterested in her story about how they had it all wrong and she owed nothing. And her landlord started making noises about evicting her because her credit was no good.

Roberta was lucky enough to find one of the few lawyers that would work on a case like hers, using connections she had at the paper. She wonders if the average person would have been able to do anything about being ripped off, because it was very difficult even for her, using her insider press status, to find representation. The lawyer she finally found told her that there was a penalty of from $100 to $1,000 for each account opened in her name without her permission and that if the case went to trial and the card companies lost, they would have to pay his reasonable fees, which could quickly mount up to many thousands of dollars. With that as a threat, the lawyer filed a suit against the companies that had opened the fraud accounts and was able to quickly settle the case. The incident took its toll on Roberta. She had always prided herself on having top-notch credit and was astounded at how quickly it had faded away. But the companies did pay enough in settlement to cover her legal bills and to leave a couple of thousand dollars over for Roberta. She wasn't able to buy an ermine coat with it, but it did suffice for the down payment on her new convertible.

---

### • CREDIT CARD INSIDER'S TIPS • ON AVOIDING IDENTITY THEFT

- ▶ Carry very few credit cards, limit the number of open accounts you have and close (by written notice) all accounts you don't use regularly.
- ▶ Keep track of when the bills on card accounts you do use should arrive and notify the company if the bills are late.
- ▶ Fight against giving out your social security number, driver's license number, or other numbers, and absolutely do not have your social security number or license number printed on your checks.
- ▶ Lock your home mailbox or use a post office box.
- ▶ Keep your name and address out of the phone book.
- ▶ Look at your credit reports every year or so.
- ▶ Ask the credit bureaus to note in your file that no account in your name is to be opened unless the credit grantor calls you and gets your okay.
- ▶ Tell the credit bureaus that you do not want your file accessed for prescreened credit offers.
- ▶ Ask the credit bureaus to take your credit information off-line.
- ▶ Keep a photocopy of all your credit cards filed away at home so that if they are stolen you can quickly notify the companies.
- ▶ Tear to shreds all credit card applications, preapproved or not, that come in the mail with your name on them and flush the shreds down the toilet.

---

# Preapproved Cards

> Mail offers for so-called "preapproved" cards may omit crucial details found in the agreement, which come later and may go unread.
> —from "Avoid the Credit Card Blues," a brochure
> by Texas Attorney General Dan Morales

Where do they get your name for all those junk-mail credit card solicitations that plague your mailbox? Mostly, these tree-destroying solicitations come from the card companies taking a peek at your credit report at one of the big three credit reporting agencies: Experian (formerly TRW), TransUnion, and Equifax.

But the federal Fair Credit Reporting Act says that nobody can look at your credit report unless they have a reasonable expectation of engaging in a credit transaction with you. That doesn't sound too hard on the companies, but the implications can be serious—so serious that the companies went to Congress and got some changes made in the Fair Credit Reporting Act (effective October 1, 1997) that lets them do some things that used to be illegal.

The companies are red-hot to send out the solicitations to line up what they think would be very profitable, creditworthy new cardholders. So, way before the 1997 changes to the law, after some political and legal juggling, the Federal Trade Commission and various federal banking regulators such as the rather well-hidden Federal Financial Institution Examination Council (FFIEC) boiled things down a bit to more or less allow what the bankers call prescreening.

Here's part of what obscure (but powerful) FFIEC said about prescreening back in the early nineties:

FFIEC Policy Statement—
Prescreening by Financial Institutions
and the Fair Credit Reporting Act

Prescreening is a process by which a consumer credit reporting agency (credit bureau) compiles or edits a list of consumers meeting specific credit granting criteria provided by an institution [institution equals credit card company]. The list is provided to the institution or a third party acting for the institution (for example, a mailing service) for use in soliciting specific consumers for credit products.

Is a Prescreen a Consumer Report?

A prescreened list represents a series of consumer reports [credit reports], since the list conveys that each consumer named on the list meets certain criteria for creditworthiness.

Is a Prescreen Permissible Under the FCRA?

[here's where it gets interesting] While the Fair Credit Reporting Act (FCRA) *does not expressly authorize it*, prescreening is permissible if the institution follows certain rules. The act permits prescreening if the institution makes a *firm offer of credit* to each consumer whose name appears on the prescreened list.

A reasonable interpretation of the above is that the FFIEC said prescreening was probably illegal, but we're going to let credit card companies do it anyway. That's pretty serious stuff for a federal agency that is supposed to uphold the law. I wonder how much pressure from lobbyists and bank lawyers it took to get those conservative bureaucratic types on the council to sign off on this incredible "policy statement", which could be interpreted as saying something like: "To hell with Congress, let's rewrite the law so the card companies like it better."

In any case, here's how prescreening works right now. A card company has a list of a million names and addresses that it bought from a mailing list company, compiled from phone books, driver's license records, voter registration cards, or whatever. The company wants to know which of those names meet its credit criteria. So it goes to another company (let's call it Banking Assistance Division, Inc., or BAD). BAD takes the names and gives them to one of the credit bureaus, which then compares the information in each person's credit report against the card company's criteria as given it by BAD—for instance, people on the name list who have only department store credit cards and haven't been more than one month late on any payments on these cards. Next, BAD gets a list back of the folks who meet the criteria and sends out the card company's preapproved solicitation to those folks.

The card company theoretically never knows which people meet its credit criteria until they return the solicitation to it (because BAD gets the names and does the mailing). Thus, the claim is, it hasn't really accessed the credit reports of the folks at issue.

But as part of this effort to get around the law restricting who can look at your credit report to folks you might actually be doing credit business with (thus keeping, for example, detectives or someone who might be thinking about suing you from looking at the personal information in your credit report), the card company *must* give a card to everyone whose credit information was accessed and who sends back the solicitation.

That was *must*, not "if we feel like it"—no asking for additional information, no demanding income tax returns if you're self-employed, no saying "our criteria have changed" or any other evasive tactics. Exceptions are granted if the preapproved person is in prison or has gone bankrupt since the prescreening was done. Even so, some companies sent out preapproved solicitations and then claimed a right to cancel the offer. For example, around half a million preapproved Discover Card solicitations were sent out in 1991–92, but, early in 1992 Discover decided to revoke the offer, claiming computer error.

So while many card companies were hot to prescreen because they think it's a very profitable way to net new customers, they are sometimes not so enthused about living up to their obligations to the folks whose credit information was accessed and whose privacy was intruded upon in the prescreening.

One way some companies have tried to have their cake and eat it, too, is to make statements suggesting that you have to do something or meet some requirements to get the preapproved card. They put on the solicitations something along the lines of:

> I certify that my household income is $30,000 or greater; that I have been, and that I am presently, current with all my creditors; and that there are no liens or judgments against me personally or professionally. I am not now, nor have I ever been bankrupt or had any part of any account written off by a creditor as not collectible. I understand that if these conditions are met, I will receive a credit card account.

Does this statement on a prescreened solicitation comply with the law? Not to my way of thinking.

Anyhow, who could possibly truthfully certify that they had never had any part of any account written off? It's nearly impossible to remember every transaction in your personal financial history. I have serious doubts about whether the card company can legally ask you to sign.

But as many card companies are hot to prescreen, not so hot to live up to their legal obligations, they, I think, throw weaselly, illegal things in their solicitations so they can try to wiggle out of their promise later on, with no concern for what the law requires.

Will the 1997 changes in prescreening requirements make a difference here? It's unclear at the time of this writing, but the changes in the law apparently will now make prescreening legal and perhaps allow some sorts of "post-screening." An example would be if the company sets up the criteria for another look at folks responding to the solicitations after they send back the preapproved form before the prescreen is done. This could open the door to widespread abuse. The changes in prescreening law effective in October 1997 appear to be leading to serious abuses of access to consumers' credit reports. The companies now claim they are able to verify information such as income used to select the folks who sent back the prescreened solicitations, and then if those folks don't meet the screening criteria, the card company may be able to pull out of its promise.

To my innocent mind, preapproved means preapproved. To a lot of card companies, it means nothing at all. What the courts will say preapproved means after the changes in the law will be up in the air for several years. I suspect that some card companies will end up losing some very expensive court cases because they have a hard time understanding what preapproved means and living up to their promises. But I also suspect that some companies will make a calculation that breaking the law is sometimes more profitable than obeying it.

# 13

# Credit Card Cops

The Democratic National Committee organized a coffee meeting at the White House last May in which some of the nation's most prominent bankers met to discuss banking regulation with President Clinton, a senior banking regulator [Eugene Ludwig, the Comptroller of the Currency], the Treasury Secretary and the top fund-raiser for the Democratic Party . . .

The guest list had been suggested by Frank N. Newman, the Bankers Trust chairman and chief executive who served earlier in the Administration as the Deputy Treasury Secretary. . . . Banking executives have been pressing the Administration to change regulations and laws.

—Stephen Labaton in *The New York Times*

While a thief who walks into a bank with a note for a teller and gets less than $1,000 faces a relentless hunt by the FBI and up to twenty years in prison, a bank president who misappropriates $1 million is usually asked by the regulatory agency to sign an agreement which in effect says, "Please don't do this anymore."

—Professor Mary L. King in *The Great American Banking SNAFU*

Banking regulators are way too influenced by the industry they supposedly regulate and do a lousy job of protecting consumers. The influence of the bankers emanates up to and down from the very highest level, the White House.

## Credit Card Cops—Their Real Job

> They [bank regulators] don't do a very good job and they never have. . . . They protect the banking system and not the public.
>
> —Professor G. J. Benston
> of the University of Rochester
> in *The New York Times*

The real job of most of the credit card cops is to protect the credit card companies. The quotes at the beginning of this chapter offer some insight into how this happens.

The most common credit cards are put out by banks and by savings and loan companies. The cops, such as the Federal Reserve Board and the Federal Home Loan Bank Board, have been told by Congress to make sure that the banks and savings and loans obey the credit card laws. But the cops have another job they think is a lot more important. That job is to keep the banks and S&Ls from going broke and maybe to help keep the party in power from going broke, too. It is not a simple job to keep the banks solvent what with all the dubious financial schemes these days.

There are other reasons the credit card cops go along with the credit card crooks, beyond the political ones. No credit card *user* is going to offer a credit card cop a high-paying job when the cop leaves the force. But an ex-cop can get a big salary when he joins up with a credit card company he was supposed to be policing while on the public payroll. Perhaps if the cop is too tough on the credit card companies he will not be offered that large salary when he leaves public service.

And the credit card companies have tons of expensive lobbyists and lawyers watching and soft-soaping the cops and their bosses. Not too many credit card users can afford to hire a law firm to influence the way regulations are written, or to be sure the cops rightfully enforce the law. Very few card users are invited to the White House for a fund-raising coffee with the president and bigwig banking regulator, Comptroller of the Currency Eugene Ludwig, as *The New York Times* reported was done for some of the biggest card companies in the country: Bank of America, NationsBank, Chase Manhattan, BancOne, and Wells Fargo.

But it's not just having your boss meet with the people you are supposed to be regulating that undermines the cops' desire and ability to protect consumers from credit card abuses by the card companies. The cops spend lots of time with the card company executives and very little time at all with card users. And soon they start to feel that their constant companions, the card execs, are right about most things, especially those trouble-making consumers.

> The president [Clinton] agreed that it was wrong for the nation's top banking regulator to have been invited to a White House gathering for bankers arranged by the DNC (Democratic National Committee], even as he defended his participation in the event. . . . But Clinton also said: "I don't see anything wrong with raising money for the political process."
>
> —Jonathan Peterson in the *Los Angeles Times*
>
> The guests included executives of banks that had given hundreds of thousands of dollars to the party in the past and, more to the point, were to give even more in the future. . . . The implicit message to the comptroller and any other federal official is that this person is important to the president. If he or she calls later, one would do well to take the call and listen carefully.
>
> —Editorial in the *Los Angeles Times*

Until the system is changed, even under different administrations, chances are the credit card cops will still be tight with the credit card crooks. So the credit card cops are much less than totally committed to helping credit card users (that means *you!*) solve their problems with credit card companies.

## Credit Card Cops—Who Are They?

Exactly who are the credit card cops? You might think that there would be one federal agency that would enforce the credit card laws (the Credit Card Bureau of Investigation?). Not so. Instead, the enforcement of credit card laws is a complicated and confusing maze, perhaps meant to confuse and intimidate the outsider, the nonbanker, the credit card user.

Plenty of federal agencies—at least seven—are supposed to keep an eye on how the credit card companies are behaving. Plus at least fifty-one state agencies are supposed to watch them, too. Here are the federal agencies listed for you:

Comptroller of the Currency
Compliance Management
250 E Street N.W.
Washington, DC 20019
800-613-6742

Note that in over thirty tries I got only a busy signal at this phone number. I don't know if that means that hundreds and thousands of angry cardholders are calling the comptroller or if it means that the phone is kept off the hook to avoid getting complaints. In any case, I guess you'd better write to the Comptroller instead of trying to call.

Federal Deposit Insurance Corporation
Division of Compliance and Consumer Affairs
550 17th Street N.W.
Washington, DC 20429
202-898-3536
800-934-FDIC

The folks on this line actually seem interested in giving consumers some help.

Office of Thrift Supervision
Division of Consumer Affairs
1700 G Street N.W.
Washington, DC 20552
202-906-6237
800-842-6929

Federal Reserve Board
Division of Consumer and Community Affairs
20th Street and Constitution Avenue N.W.
Washington, DC 20551
202-452-3693

Federal Trade Commission
Division of Credit Practices
Washington, DC 20580
202-326-3128 or 326-3761

National Credit Union Administration
Public and Congressional Affairs
1775 Duke Street
Alexandria, VA 22314
703-518-6330

The attorney general of the United States can also chase credit card crooks, but somehow just doesn't seem to get around to it much, although under Janet Reno, the Justice Department did some investigation of Visa and MasterCard rules that prohibit Visa or MasterCard issuers from also issuing American Express Cards.

### Choosing the Right Cop
Above are the credit card cops' addresses and phone numbers. How do you know which one to contact when you have got a problem? To tell you the truth, it doesn't really matter too much.

The cops don't tell you this, but they are required to forward your complaint to the right place if you send it to the wrong agency. And *this* legal duty they gladly fulfill, for it is a way of passing along a potential problem to another agency.

Since the Federal Reserve Board is "first among equals" in the credit card regulation world, I suggest that you send your *written* complaint to them. They will more or less graciously send it to the correct agency. Or call the toll-free number, 800-934-FDIC, of the Consumer Complaint Office of the Federal Deposit Insurance Corporation in Washington. They should be able to tell you which agency regulates the credit card company that is causing you problems. Try calling the toll-free line from 9 A.M. to 4 P.M. EDT.

Or you can try to figure out the credit card cop maze yourself using the following information about the area each cop is supposed to watch.

## The Cops' Beats

Each of the regulatory agencies covers certain kinds of financial institutions.

The Comptroller of the Currency
National banks, those with "National" or "N.A." (for "National Association") in their names.
Federal Deposit Insurance Corporation
State banks that do not belong to the Federal Reserve System. How a consumer is supposed to know if a bank belongs to the Federal Reserve System is unclear.
Office of Thrift Supervision
Federally insured savings and loans or federal savings banks (often have "F.S.B." following their name).
Federal Reserve Board
State banks that belong to the Federal Reserve System—banks that do not have "National" or "N.A." in their names.
Federal Trade Commission
Department store or retail store credit cards, consumer finance companies (Household Finance, Beneficial Finance), or non-bank-type credit cards (American Express). The FTC also regulates credit bureaus and bill collectors.
National Credit Union Administration
Credit unions.

## Credit Card Cops—Can They Help You?

Given all the bad things about the credit card cops set out above, can they help you? The answer is yes.

The credit card cops do have power over the credit card companies. While they rarely use it to help consumers, a card company's fear that the cops might be goaded into action by consumer complaints can be useful to you in getting a problem resolved.

The agencies can issue reprimands or cease and desist orders and can take all sorts of other legal action against a crooked credit card company—actions that can really hurt the company.

Do the credit card cops have the desire to help you? Not really, or at least not much desire, for the reasons explained above. Even so, you may be able to use them to pressure the credit card company as discussed below.

"The agencies, if at all possible, will avoid enforcing regulations," writes one-time bank president Edward Mrkvicka, Jr. Mrkvicka, in his fine book *Battle Your Bank—And Win*, suggests that you

> ignore all avenues that are cosmetically designed to create the appearance of governmental interest or assistance. National banks have placed in the lobby booklets entitled "Do You Have a Consumer Complaint?" If you read the material you may conclude that the comptroller's [of the currency] office is ready and eager to respond to your case and champion your interest. Not so.

Mrkvicka goes on to suggest that you write *one* letter to the appropriate credit card cops, and then after you wait a reasonable length of time, contact a lawyer. In his experience a prompt response from the cops should not be expected, and neither should any help. "The bank has a distinct advantage, since it has the protection of the regulatory agencies," says Mrkvicka. I would suggest that you send your letter to the cops certified mail with a return receipt requested. The cost is a couple of dollars more than regular postage, but someone who can prove their letter was received is, I think, *much* more likely to get action from the cops.

Mrkvicka suggests that writing to the local newspaper's "Action Line" is more likely to work than going to the credit card cops. Perhaps. But I think it is sometimes possible to get action from the cops without going to "Action Line," although a letter to the press will not hurt.

I think it unlikely that the credit card cops will take serious action to solve any major credit card problems. However, filing a complaint with them may goad the credit card company into resolving the problems on its own.

In fact, the *threat* of filing a complaint may be more powerful than actually making a complaint. Why is this? Because the credit card companies like to have clean files at the regulatory agencies. If there are too many consumer complaints against them pending in the files at the agency that is supposed to watch them, somebody from the cops might actually try to find out what is going on. Unlikely, but it could happen.

Also, when Congress holds hearings on possible bills to change consumer protection laws, it often asks the banking regulators about consumer complaints in various areas. So the card companies think it a good idea to have as clean a record as possible with the regulators. Plus, someone who knows that there *are* banking regulators and knows how to complain to them is just the type of educated consumer who might actually cause some real trouble for a light-fingered credit card company.

---

### • CREDIT CARD INSIDER'S TIP •

Always threaten a troublesome credit card company *in writing* with taking your complaint to the credit card cops *before* you do it. The threat of complaining is probably more powerful than the effect the making of the complaint would have. *Mention the name of the appropriate agency in making your threat to the card company.* Send your threat to the company president.

---

Complaints to the Federal Trade Commission, which covers nonbank credit card companies, are a special case. The other credit card cops will mostly make an "investigation" of your complaint even if that investigation is just asking the credit card company to look at its records and tell the agency what happened. The FTC generally does not even do that because the FTC does not see working on individual problems as an important aspect of its job. The FTC has the power to investigate industries and issue regulations to correct illegal actions by those industries. That is, in its view, its main work. This is worthwhile work, but it does not help you much if you have a problem with American Express. However, a complaint by you to the FTC can lead to an investigation that will perhaps help correct a pattern of crooked action by a credit card company.

Often what an agency will do is send a letter to a special department at the card company that handles relations with the regulators. That special department sometimes provides special treatment for the very rare, trouble-making consumer (in the company's eyes) who knows how to complain to the regulators.

Thus a complaint to the credit card cops may help solve your problems, but do not count on it. The credit card cops—excluding the FTC—are much closer to the credit card companies than you will ever be. Even so, complaining to the cops can put pressure on the credit card companies and can be worth doing.

### Credit Card Cops—The Best Way to Complain to Them

If your attempts to work things out with the credit card company fail, here are some tips on how to effectively complain to the credit card cops:

**1.** Complain to the Washington, D.C., headquarters office rather than the local office in your region.

*Reason:* The headquarters office will forward your complaint to the local office for investigation, but there will be a record of its being received in Washington and forwarded. Sometimes complaints filed with local offices can just disappear. This is less likely to happen if the locals know the big boss in the District of Columbia knows about the complaint.

*Disadvantage:* Forwarding your complaint from Washington to a local office can add a week or two onto the time it takes to get the investigation under way in the local office.

**2.** Complain in writing. You can telephone a complaint in, but you are not likely to get very far.

*Reason:* The federal government runs on paper. For lots of government folks, if it is not written down, it does not exist. And if your complaint is written, the credit card cops know that it's likely you have a copy. A phone complaint is easier to ignore than a written one.

**3.** Send your complaint letter certified mail, return receipt requested.

*Reason:* With a return receipt—staple it to the back of your copy of the letter when the mailman brings it back to you—you can prove that the credit card cops got the complaint and when they got it. This will almost certainly get you a quicker response.

**4.** Put on the bottom of the letter itself "Certified mail No. xxxxxxxxx—return receipt requested." (The number to use is on the certification form; each such form is individually numbered.)

*Reason:* To let the person handling the complaint know that you can prove the letter was received by the cops. That way it may be less likely to get "lost."

**5.** If you do not get any serious action out of the credit card cops, try complaining to your congressperson (name and address available from the reference desk at your local public library).

*Reason:* An inquiry from your representative to the credit card cops may give them the boot they need to *seriously* tackle your complaint. It also gives your representative the idea that neither the credit card companies nor the credit card cops are doing what they should. Maybe this will help get Congress to take action to correct the evil ways of the companies and the credit card cops.

# 14

# Sue Your Credit Card Company: When, Why, and How

Just remember this: if bankers were as smart as you are, you would starve to death.
—Lawyer Henry Harfield, senior partner in Wall Street law firm Shearman & Sterling, talking to a lawyers' group. Quoted in *The Bankers* by Martin Mayer.

This might have been the hardest chapter in this book to write, because I have to tell you several almost contradictory things about the legal system. I want to tell you that the court system stands ready, able, and willing to leap to your defense when your consumer rights as a credit card user are violated. Sort of.

After all, Congress and many state legislatures have passed very potent laws to protect you against predatory acts by the card companies. And those laws give you apparently powerful and special rights, such as getting your lawyer's fees paid by the card company when you win your court case. This is exactly the opposite of the usual rule in American courts, which is that both sides in a lawsuit have to pay for their own lawyers, no matter which side wins the case. This is a terrific weapon for consumers. Congress decided that consumers and their lawyers needed extra incentive to go to court on credit card rip-offs. The card companies have lawyers on retainer. Consumers do not.

I also have to tell you that things are not as great for consumers as they might seem at first glance. You may have big problems finding a lawyer to take on your credit card case, even if it is well justified, since many lawyers, for some good reasons, believe that they often aren't paid enough in consumer cases to make it worth all the work. But you may well be able to get around those problems, get your case prosecuted anyhow, and win a valuable consumer victory.

It's true, the laws Congress and the state legislatures wrote do give you powerful credit card rights. And it's true, you can go to court to enforce them. But there are obstacles, many created by pro-credit-card company, anti-consumer judges who under our common law system have a whale of a lot of power when it comes to enforcing laws. And the only place you can go to get laws enforced is in front of a judge.

The biggest obstacle is that anti-consumer judges have been making it more and more difficult for your lawyer in a credit card case to get paid what he or she would make putting in the same time and effort in another kind of case. One way those judges have made it difficult for you to get your lawyer's fees paid is to refuse to award you your attorney's fees when the money you recover for the company's violations is *de minimus,* or not very much (although what's not very much to a judge who mostly spends his time on big corporate cases may be big bucks to a consumer). Since most credit card cases brought by consumers do not result in big damage awards at trial, a judge's failure to award you your attorney's fees in card cases where you only get a few hundred or a thousand dollars from the card company means your lawyer takes a pretty big risk of not getting paid or of fighting for months or years for less than enough money to pay the office overhead. This makes it tougher for consumers to find lawyers. Of course the card companies don't have the same problems, having plenty of well-paid corporate lawyers at their beck and call.

Thus, although Congress said you should recover your reasonable attorney's fees in a credit card case, some anti-consumer judges have cooked up ways to keep your lawyer from getting paid. This matters a lot because lawyers, like most everyone, need to get paid for their work. And contrary to the corporate propaganda put out so assiduously by well-paid hacks, lawyers who work to protect credit card users' rights are not vastly overpaid.

So it may be tough to find a credit card lawyer to take your case. But it's certainly not impossible.

Why would you *want* to sue the bank or card company that sold you your credit card? Because that is what should be done when you have a problem neither the credit card company nor the credit card cops will solve for you.

You should go straight to court. In fact, you don't have much choice. If after a serious, written effort to get the problem corrected, it is still a problem, then you either go to court or you decide to live with the problem.

## How to Sue a Credit Card Company

Congress gave you the right to sue credit card companies on your own for breaking the credit card laws. You can on your very own (with the help of a lawyer) take a credit card company to court. Plus, you can make money while you make the company obey the law. There is no legal requirement to complain to the credit card cops first, although it probably will not do any harm to try them—as long as you do not expect much real help from them. Perhaps Congress, in its wisdom, lacked trust in both the credit card companies and the credit card cops, and so left this opening for you?

Here is really good news for folks who have problems with a credit card company and have to go to court. *When you win, the credit card company pays your lawyer!*

Let's repeat that. When you win a lawsuit against a credit card company, federal law requires that the company pay your lawyer. This is a tremendously strong tool for you to use against a credit card company that gets out of legal line.

Why is making the credit card company pay your lawyer such a powerful tool for you? Because the harder the credit card company fights you, the more it will have to pay your lawyer if it loses. And even if it settles the case without going to trial, the company can still be made to pay your lawyer's fees.

This gives the company a really good reason to quickly straighten out things with you. Even a brief courtroom battle with you can easily cost the company $25,000—$15,000 for their lawyer, $10,000 for your lawyer (somehow, credit card company lawyers always seem to make more on a case than the consumer lawyer, and I don't think it's because they work harder), plus whatever the company has to pay you for its wrongdoing. Once you have a lawyer file suit, the company has a strong incentive to resolve things fast and would be smart to do so (of course, as you know by now, some card companies are not too smart).

Who pays your lawyer if you lose? Why, he just does not get paid. At least that's the theory. The reality may be a bit different. Because it is sometimes difficult for lawyers to get paid what they should in cases where the lawyer's fees are awarded by the judge after the lawyer has won the case for a consumer, many consumer lawyers want some money up-front from the consumer. This also has the desirable effect (from the lawyer's point of view) of discouraging the occasional person who comes to a lawyer with the idea that he will hit the jackpot on the case without any commitment of money or time on his part.

Perhaps the most common way of paying your lawyer in consumer protection cases is to put up some money up-front and agree to pay the lawyer a portion of any damages awarded, as well as the court-awarded attorney's fees. If the lawyer gets paid only when he wins the case for you, that's called a contingency fee. The fee is contingent on the lawyer's winning the case. But you may not be able to find a lawyer to take your case on a strict contingency fee basis. It is not unreasonable for the lawyer to ask for some money up-front to cover the case-filing fee, other expenses, and some of the time he or she will put in on the case.

By the way, if you are broke, most court systems allow you to file a case *in forma pauperis*—that is, as a pauper, or someone who can't afford the court fees and also pay for food and rent. But you have to search out how to do this. The clerk at the courthouse is not likely to volunteer that it can be done.

Here in California the clerk of the court is required to give out the forms to proceed *in forma pauperis* for free to anyone who asks. But you have to ask or your lawyer has to ask for you.

Why would a lawyer agree to proceed on a contingency fee? A smart lawyer will not take a case on a contingency fee basis unless he is rather sure it is a winner. So if a lawyer will take your case on a contingency fee basis, you probably have a winning case. If you can't find a lawyer to take the case on at least a partially contingent fee, you probably should not be in court anyway.

You may have to try many lawyers to find one who sees the true merits of your case and also knows something about credit card law. Don't give up if a couple of lawyers don't want your case. Some folks have had to call thirty or more lawyers to find one who wanted to handle their case on a contingency basis.

Many credit card rights cases tend to be fairly easy to settle. The evidence of the card company's wrongdoing is usually all down in black and white. This makes it easier for your lawyer to show that the company was bad.

Unfortunately, most lawyers don't know much about credit card law. And attorneys, as is true of almost everyone, do not like to deal with the completely unfamiliar. Most lawyers know that the client and the lawyer can both do okay in a car accident case, but they are not so sure about a credit card rights case. So you may have a considerable search on your hands to find a lawyer who is willing to take on your credit card problem, even if he or she stands to make some very good money off the case. In fact, one of the reasons I wrote this book was to make everyone, *including* lawyers, more aware of the profitable possibilities of suing misbehaving credit card companies. After all, the only way we'll ever get them to behave is if we make them pay for their bad behavior.

Let's assume you have found a lawyer to handle your case against the credit card company. When you hire a lawyer to handle a credit card case, be sure that the written fee agreement (an agreement in writing is required by law in some states and an excellent idea in the other states) sets things up on at least a partial contingent fee basis.

### *You Have Only a Year*

There is a time limit on your right to sue credit card companies. Federal law says you have to do it within a year (in a few cases, two years) of the time the credit card company did its illegal stuff to you. Otherwise, except if the company sues you to try and collect some money, you may not be able to successfully sue it over its nasty deeds. Some state laws may give you more than a year for some kinds of problems, but there may be problems in using the state laws. So why not act within a year and get the advantages of using federal law?

If you have problems with a credit card company, do not let those problems ride. A year can go by awfully fast and you may lose out. Some kinds of credit card law-breaking by card companies do have a two-year time limit. One of those is the Equal Credit Opportunity Act (15 U.S.C. 1691). Ask a lawyer about it if there is a problem with the one-year time limit.

Remember, it can take several months to find a lawyer and get a lawsuit filed, so do not wait for months after the dirty deeds of the company are done to get going. If you do wait too long, you may find you have struck out without ever getting to the plate. Take action!

## Finding the Right Lawyer

Finding a good lawyer to take on your case is probably the hardest part of suing a credit card company. As Boston attorney Mark Leymaster says in *The Business Lawyer,* "I've noticed that there is so much consumer law and so many consumer lawyers, but so few lawyers for consumers." The lawyer you deal with need not be a specialist in credit card law. And a good thing too, because most of the specialists work for the credit card companies. If you know of or have a lawyer you have reason to trust, then he or she may be the one for you. Being comfortable with and trusting your lawyer may be more important than his or her knowledge of a certain, specialized area.

If you do not have a lawyer in mind, try these things.

• Call one or more of the law schools in your area and ask for the dean's office. Then ask the dean's secretary who in the school teaches the classes on consumer credit or is knowledgeable about consumer credit. Call up that professor, tell him what you are up to, and ask for him to recommend a few attorneys for you to contact. Maybe one of the professor's former students is now practicing consumer-oriented law.

• Call the legal clinic at the law schools (the dean's secretary will probably come through on this one, too) and ask who is in charge of consumer credit cases. That person probably knows every lawyer in town who handles consumer credit cases.

• Check the index of your local newspaper under such categories as "credit," "credit cards," "consumer rights," and "banking" for stories along the lines of "Consumer gets $27,000 from Last National Bank." An Internet search of newspaper back issues might also be useful if your local paper is Net-accessible (call the paper and ask). Then, note who the lawyer is in any cases you find and call that person up. If the lawyer is not named in the story, call the reporter at the paper or the consumer who got the $27,000 and ask who handled the case.

• Call the local Legal Services (poverty law) office. The local bar association, law school library, or county law library reference desk ought to be able to tell you where it is. Or ask your congressperson's local office for help in finding it.

Legal Services is filled with dedicated, consumer-oriented lawyers who usually know more than most about credit card law. They might be able to handle your case if you are not too well off, or the person at the local office who handles consumer credit cases may know a knowledgeable lawyer in private practice whom he or she can recommend.

• Call the local newspapers and ask for the legal reporter. Reporters love to talk, and the legal ones had better know something about a lot of lawyers. Ask for the names of a few who handle consumer credit cases or who are extra-aggressive.

If you live in a big city there is probably a specialized legal newspaper. You can find out if there is one by calling the reference desk at a local law library or perhaps by asking the reference librarian at the public library. Often the special legal paper is for sale at the newsstand at the main courthouse in town. Reporters for such a paper often know all about the local lawyers. Call up a reporter whose name you find in the paper and ask for his or her help in locating a good consumer lawyer.

• Contact the National Lawyers Guild. The guild, which is definitely *not* like the establishment American Bar Association, is a group of lawyers who describe themselves as progressive. The members tend to be much more interested in consumer problems than the average lawyer. The guild has offices in most big cities and members in many more places. Check the telephone white pages directory in the nearest big city for a listing. The guild does not have a formal referral system, but the executive director in your city may be able to give you the names of some local members who might consider taking your case.

• Contact the National Association of Consumer Advocates, 18 Tremont St., Boston, Mass. 02109, 617-723-1239. This is a fairly new group of (mostly) lawyers with members (including me) around the country. They may be able to help you connect with a consumer-oriented lawyer in your area.

The local bar association almost always has a referral service for folks looking for a lawyer. Usually the set-up is something like this: You pay $20 or so and get the names of three lawyers who have signed up for referrals. Your money buys you the right to a half-hour consultation with one of the three. Generally the referral service cannot provide you with lawyers who specialize in an area that you request. I suggest you avoid these programs, not because you cannot get a good lawyer through them, but because I think your chances of finding an attorney right for your credit card needs are better using the other approaches in this section.

While you are looking for a lawyer keep in mind that almost all lawyers will gladly talk to someone who calls and says "I am a prospective client" to the secretary. Lawyers may, if they do not know you, try to evaluate your case right on the phone. So be ready when you call. Have the facts in your case fresh in your mind. And be ready to sum up your problem in a short conversation of five minutes or so. Be sure to mention that you want this case taken on at least a partial contingency fee basis.

Do not be embarrassed to call up lawyers you do not know and ask for their help. Lawyers generally love to gab, and they also like to make money. To do that they need clients at least as much as you need a lawyer.

Should you do it yourself? No, NO, *NO!* Do *not* go down to small-claims court and sue the credit card company yourself. Going to small-claims court is a good idea when you have a consumer problem and the money involved is too little to justify hiring a lawyer. But this does not apply to credit card cases, because the credit card company will pay for your lawyer (when you win), no matter how small the sum you sue over.

---

**• CREDIT CARD INSIDER'S TIP •**

Look out!!! A lawsuit can be a time-consuming, emotionally draining experience. Do not embark on one unless you are really provoked and ready for a long, exhausting battle. On the other hand, to quote Davy Crockett by way of Walt Disney, "be sure you're right, then go ahead."

---

Often, what the credit card company pays the lawyer is a lot more than what they have to pay you. So if you get a lawyer, the company knows it will get socked harder. So it settles faster, saving you time and trouble.

I have seen too many folks who filed a case in small-claims court and messed up what could have been a very good case. If your case goes to trial in small-claims court you usually don't have any right to appeal or to bring your claims against the same credit card company in the regular court system.

I love the idea of small-claims court—folks informally having their minor disputes resolved—but in my experience, small-claims court is rarely the place for a credit card case. Going to small-claims court in credit card matters is like tying both hands behind your back just before getting into the ring for the championship bout. Don't do it.

## Arbitration—Bad for Consumers

A few card companies have thought up a wonderful new way to try and avoid being sued. They put an arbitration clause is their small-print contracts that you don't get until *after* your new account is opened. That arbitration clause keeps you (at least in the card company's view) from making it go to court if it wrongs you. Instead, you have to go before a purportedly neutral arbitrator, you don't get your constitutional right to a jury trial, and you're just plain knocked out of the court system. In the end, it turns out to be great for the card companies, much less than great for the card user.

I'm especially impressed by the anti-consumer plan of Circuit City Stores, Inc.'s wholly owned bank, First North American National Bank, which issues both Circuit City credit cards and regular credit cards. A clause in an application I saw says that all disputes will be arbitrated, but all disputes over $5,000 must be arbitrated in Richmond, Virginia. This is useful for the card company, but not so useful if you buy a $6,000 computer in San Francisco and it refuses to compute. You refuse to pay the card bill and now you are supposed to go to Richmond, perhaps 3,000 miles away, for an arbitration hearing a few blocks from Circuit City's headquarters. This sounds like an unfair and deceptive practice to me. In fact, ITT's consumer finance company got socked very hard in a case involving its efforts to force folks in California to go to Minnesota for arbitration before an arbitration company that had some very close ties to the ITT subsidiary. I understand that ITT is now out of that aspect of the consumer finance business.

Theoretically, arbitration sounds great: cut through the legal mumbo jumbo and let a neutral arbitrator straighten things out. This sounds great but isn't. Many think that the arbitrators aren't so neutral. In fact, they may even be pro card company, because they depend on repeat business from the card companies for their bread and butter—indeed, often, their entire livelihood.

Arbitration would be okay if it were *voluntary*, if both sides agreed to it *when there was a problem*. And that's always possible, even without any arbitration clause in the agreement. But it's not okay to try and force consumers into arbitration by hiding a mandatory arbitration clause in an agreement that almost no one reads and thereby depriving them of their constitutional right to have any problems heard by a jury of their peers.

This situation cries out for some new law. Let's hope we get it, because without the controls the jury system can put on card companies, who knows what they might do.

## Good Consumer's Complaint Letters

Here are some sample letters sent and received by A Good Consumer. Sometimes a *politely* threatening letter to the right card company officer can be very effective. And you don't have to go to court to send a certified letter; just make a trip to the post office.

> 123 Sycamore Place
> Sierra, CA 99999
> 26 August, 2002

John Roe, Chairman and Chief Executive Officer
SouthEast Iowa-Illinois Bank
Couchport, Iowa 55555

Dear President Roe:

This letter concerns some of SEII Bank's subsidiary corporations that you should be aware of and want to rectify before I seek other remedies.

In May of 2001, I made a purchase of machinery with my Monster-Vista card #1234567890, issued by Card Issuing Issuers of Moline, Illinois, a subsidiary of SEII Bank. The machinery was not as represented and so I filed a charge-back claim within the appropriate time. The charge-back was not honored and SEII Bank reported me delinquent to credit reporting agencies without notifying me and without noting that the sum in question was in dispute. In addition to reporting the situation incorrectly, SEII Bank listed the "charge off" twice, giving me two blemishes on my otherwise spotless credit record. Various other actions by SEII Bank and Card Issuing Issuers have caused me a good deal of grief and interfered with the peace of my household and my ability to do business.

My letters to Card Issuing Issuers have been ignored.

I have consulted with an attorney expert in credit card law and have been informed that a number of laws have been violated by your people in this matter. Before hiring a lawyer to rectify my situation, I would like to know if you would simply arrange for SEII Bank to erase the detrimental and incorrect notations completely from my credit report files so that my otherwise clean credit record is restored. I am certain you can understand this means a great deal to me.

If you investigate the matter, you will see that things have been done that do not reflect well on SEII Bank and which the bank regulatory agencies and state authorities regard with disfavor.

There are time limits I understand I must obey, so if I do not hear from you by September 10, 2002, I will assume you are not interested in cleaning up the situation.

Sincerely,

A. Good Consumer

Certified Mail # P0987654321—Return Receipt Requested
cc: Pres. John O'Malley, Card Issuing Issuers, Inc., 1000 Vista Drive, Moline, IL
Pres. Sally Haveaheart, MonsterVista Card, 666 East Michigan Blvd., Suite 666, Chicago, IL 66666

MonsterVista Card
666 East Michigan Boulevard
Chicago, Illinois 66666
September 30, 2002

Mr. A. Good Consumer
123 Sycamore Place
Sierra, CA 99999

Dear Mr. Good Consumer:

This is in response to your recent letter sent to Sally "Bootsie" Haveaheart, president of MonsterVista Card, concerning your SEII Bank MonsterVista Card and your dispute with Big Crock, Inc. Your letter had been forwarded to me for follow up.

Upon receipt of your letter I contacted SEII Bank and asked them to review the circumstances concerning your dispute with the merchant and to determine if the dispute was handled properly.

SEII Bank and Card Issuer Issuers, Inc., has just advised me that they have concluded their investigation and based upon their findings have brought the balance down to $0 on your MonsterVista Card account and deleted any reference to the account from credit bureau reports.

Please accept my apologies for any inconvenience this may have caused you, and I hope that MonsterVista Card continues to be your card of choice in the future.

Sincerely,
James Smooth
Director, Product Service & Delivery

cc: Sally "Bootsie" Haveaheart

SEII Bank
Executive Offices
Couchport, Iowa 55555
September 28, 2002

Mr. A Good Consumer
123 Sycamore Place
Sierra, CA 99999

Dear Mr. Good Consumer:

I am writing to you concerning your recent letter dated August 26, 2002, addressed to Chairman and CEO John Roe.

When a customer is involved in a dispute such as yours, we make every possible attempt to assist them in resolving their situation. However, we are governed by strict rules and regulations established by MonsterVista Card. When our office was originally contacted regarding this matter, an attempt was made to credit your account for the disputed charges from Big Crock, Inc. As you are aware from our previous correspondence, this attempt was not successful.

After thoroughly reviewing your situation again, we have determined that your special case warranted further evaluation. I have included a breakdown of your dispute, as our office has it on record, for your review [copy of breakdown not reproduced here].

In summary, we find that because we cannot verify certain information in your case, we will take the following steps:

1. Bring the account to a $0 balance.
2. Delete our trade line from your credit bureau reports.

It is extremely important to the success of our business to receive feedback from our customers. From this feedback we can strive to be proactive in our effort to meet each customer's wants and needs. I sincerely apologize for the inconvenience this matter has caused and thank you for bringing it to our attention.

Sincerely,
Barbara Oily, Director, Credit Card Operations

cc: John Roe

# 15

# The Internet
# and Credit Cards

The Internet provides a valuable way for you to gather credit card information and a futuristic way for credit crooks to come right into your home and rip you off from a net server in, perhaps, the Bahamas or Thailand—anywhere beyond easy reach of American law enforcement. Positively, the Net provides computer-using card users with ways to seek out information such as up-to-date data about card costs. It's easy to search the Net and find many sites offering credit card information, including sites that allow you to search various databases for deals that match your criteria and sites that provide lists of low-rate and low-fee cards, including secured cards.

I do have a warning about much of the information you find on the Net. While the rate and fee information I've seen is generally pretty accurate and useful, much of the other card information on the Net, particularly information about the legal rights of card users, is just plain wrong. I can't say "buyer beware" because you're not buying the information. But I do say "Net surfer beware." Nobody is checking on the Internet to ensure that the information posted is correct. At least if you read something in a magazine you know that an editor looked at the information before it was published. Anyone can go on the Net and say anything.

Here are a few of the sites with card information on them. No doubt, in the chaotic world of the Net, many of these sites will have changed by the time you read this, but a little looking with a search engine such as AltaVista (www.altavista.digital.com) or Yahoo (www.yahoo.com) should glean you plenty of information, good and bad. Yahoo has useful collections of credit site addresses its staff has gathered. I would start my search with Yahoo. I would also keep in mind that Visa International has a $21 million ownership stake in Yahoo, although to date there's nothing to suggest that the Visa stake has any effect on Yahoo searches.

*Bank Rate Monitor*
www.bankrate.com   Plenty of information including lots of low-rate and low-fee cards. This site is put together by a well-known banking publication.

*CardFinder*
www.getsmart.com   A site with some useful information. Presently limited to cards from the bigger banks.

*Credit Choice*
www.creditchoice.com   This site is operated by Internet Access Financial Corporation (IAFC). I have no further information about IAFC, but did find some useful information on this site.

*Federal Reserve Board*
www.bog.frb.fed.us   The official site of the Federal Reserve Board contains, among many other interesting pieces of information, the Fed's half-yearly survey of annual fees, interest rates, etc., for most large banks in the country.

*Federal Trade Commission*
www.ftc.gov   The official site of the FTC has copies of many pamphlets on consumer credit, including credit cards and plenty of other consumer information as well.

*Privacy Rights Clearinghouse*
www.privacyrights.org   Excellent information on privacy issues regarding consumer credit, social security numbers, and many other areas.

*Public Interest Research Groups*
www.pirg.org   This site is full of good consumer information, including reports on identity theft and credit problems. Also lists PIRG groups around the country you can contact if you want to work for reforms in the credit system.

*Ram Research*

> www.cardtrak.com   Lists plenty of card offers. This site is from a banking industry research company that also puts out the printed low fee and rate guide *Cardtrak*, which it sells for $5.

Now, let's look at some of the credit card problems you can have on the Net.

> Your worst nightmares about the Internet are already coming true. . . . [T]he Office of the Comptroller of the Currency issued an alert about an unchartered institution on the Web that attempted to solicit deposits from unwitting consumers via the Internet. This bogus bank, Freedom Star National Bank of Arizona, is at least the third phony institution that the OCC has nailed on the Internet.
>
> "It's easy to duplicate someone else's site and create your own bogus site," notes David Stewart, director at Global Concepts, Inc., Atlanta. "I'm not a hacker, but in ten minutes, you could build a site that replicates an existing Web site of a bank."
>
> —Jackie Cohen in *Bank Technology News*

Your card number can be stolen and used for fraudulent charges when you send it over the Net to what you think is a legitimate site. For example, in a *New York Times* story, "Bogus Web Sites Troll for Credit Card Numbers," Peter Wayner reports that fake Websites are set up using the identity of legitimate companies to solicit orders (which will never be filled) and collect customer identity information and credit card numbers that will then be used for fraudulent purchases.

Tom Van Hare of Capstone Studio, a Net site designer, told Wayner that he had come across more than thirty-five such fake Websites. Most, said Hare, appear to have been set up to steal card numbers.

Even the FBI has been victimized. The FBI computer crime unit found a Website that promised (for a fee charged to your credit card) the impossible: to find any FBI files on yourself within forty-eight hours. The only way to get your FBI file is to make a Freedom of Information Act request and wait for many, many months for the FBI to respond. This can't be done over the Internet. And it certainly can't be done by non-FBI folks who put up a Net site claiming to be the FBI.

Your card number can be stolen from the computer of a company that has come by it legitimately—say, your bank or a reputable company you have done business with. Thus, Net subscribers to two very popular Websites, those of the National Basketball Association and ESPN Sports, got an anonymous E-mail message telling them that their card numbers had been stolen. Starwave Corporation, the operator of the two services, said that its security had been broken and 2,397 customers had had their card numbers stolen. The anonymous message said, "You are the victim of a careless abuse of privacy and security," and claimed to be sent by an anonymous group looking to make the Net safe for business. Each message included the last eight numbers of the receiver's card number.

Credit card companies appear to be very vulnerable to theft of card numbers and other customer information over the Internet as well. Dan Farmer, an independent security consultant, reports on a study he did in late 1996 (www.trouble.org/survey),which found security problems in 68.33 percent of the 660 bank host computers and 51.07 percent of credit union hosts nonintrusively scanned over the Net. According to Farmer, many of the insecure host computers are essentially wide open to any knowledgeable hacker ten to twelve seconds after the hacker dials up the host. And of course, the most successful Net frauds are those that haven't yet been discovered.

There are also plenty of just plain old-fashioned frauds on the Net, as well as some new twists that are possible only on the Net. Typical of the old-time frauds given new life on the Net are the endless E-mail messages sent out to millions of Netizens promising things like "Big Money, Fast & Easy—takes just ten minutes a month!" if you send $10 to a post office box in New York City, or offering to let you work at home addressing envelopes at $5 each (send just $29.95 for your start-up kit—guaranteed refundable—to Suite 1, Rip-off, CA).

More interesting, and just as potentially costly, are the Net-specific scams. Stephen Frank of *The Wall Street Journal* investigated an offshore (meaning issued outside the United States) credit card, a multilevel marketing plan built around the notion that you can charge anything you want on its offshore card (with guaranteed approval of all applicants, even bankrupts) and, with perfect legality, never pay the charges back, apparently because the plan claims that as you sign up new applicants you get credit for fees and payments by the newbies. All it costs is $100 up-front and $25 a month. For some reason, says the sponsor, the name of the bank issuing the credit card cannot be revealed, and it cannot use the names of Visa or MasterCard. This plan, says GMG Global Marketing Group, is not an illegal pyramid scheme. Thousands of people signed up for it, but soon after *The Wall Street Journal* started its investigation, its main sponsor moved to the Cayman Islands, outside the reach of U.S. law enforcement.

Says attorney Paul Luehr of the Federal Trade Commission: "We've seen potential pyramid schemes [on the Net] cover the gamut, everything from phone cards to offshore investments to membership clubs." There are so many, says Mr. Luehr, that we can't take them all to federal court.

> If you thought surfing the Net was a nameless, faceless kind of adventure—think again. Every time you visit a site—whether you're shopping or visiting X-rated sites—whatever you do there can be directly traced back to you. The tracking software included on Web browsers like Netscape and Microsoft's Explorer is called cookies.
> —Jim Goldman, reporting on KRON-TV (San Francisco)

Finally, you should be aware of the cookie problem on the Net. Not cookies like Mom bakes, but a computer program used by Internet sites called cookies—a lovable name for a not-so-lovable program. A cookie is like a passport that gets stamped when you enter a Website. The site gives it to your computer and information about the cookie is stored on your hard drive without your knowledge (unless you have the cookie security alert enabled on your browser). Using cookies, sites can track information about what sites and pages in those sites you have visited. While cookies may have valid uses, such as allowing you to enter your ID code only once for registration-required sites that you visit often, they can also seriously invade your privacy.

Cookies and other methods of tracking where you go and what you do on the Net can allow folks you have never had any contact with to know that you have, for example, visited nine sites that deal with secured credit cards for folks with credit problems, and which pages on those sites you looked at and how long you spent looking at each page. All this information is being sent over the Net, where it's not so hard to intercept it.

What should you do to protect yourself on the Net?

• Avoid giving out your credit card number on the Net. My own personal rule is to never buy anything that requires I pay for it by transmitting my card number via the Internet. The only exception is signing up for an on-line service provider, because if you don't send your number over the Net for that, you probably can't go on-line. I would be especially skeptical of claims that one site or another is "certified" secure by somebody or other.

• Activate the cookie warning on your browser (Netscape and Internet Explorer, versions 3.0 and higher) and refuse to accept cookies unless you have a good reason to do so, such as to avoid entering your user ID every time you access the site.

• Check the Net for more cookie protection information. Good places to look include the Pretty Good Privacy site (www.pgp.com), which offers PGPcookie.cutter freeware, *Wired* magazine's site (www.wired.com), or a general information site at www.cookiecentral.com.

• Be very aware that using the Net can be like using a bookstore, where every book and magazine and every page you look at may be being recorded by people you do not know for purposes you don't know.

> Keep hands and feet inside Website at all times. No electrons were harmed in the making of this Website. Don't forget to read more books.
> —Warning on bookseller Amazon.com's Website

# Resources

## How to Find Low-Fee, Low-Rate Cards

Current information on good credit card deals is published each month in *Kiplinger's Personal Finance Magazine* and in *Money*; copies are available at your local library or newsstand. Or check in your local Sunday paper. The *Los Angeles Times* and the *Chicago Sun-Times*, for example, have been running a list of good deals in their Sunday business sections.

Also, look at Chapter 15 for information about credit-card shopping on-line.

## Books

*Battle Your Bank—And Win!* (Morrow, 1985), *The Bank Book* (Harper-Collins, 1989), *Your Bank Is Ripping You Off* (St. Martin's Press, 1997), all by Edward F. Mrkvicka, Jr. Excellent books about banking problems, from a consumer perspective. Written by a former bank president. You should definitely take a look at these. *Battle Your Bank—And Win!* is out of print, so try the library.

*Charge It: Inside the Credit Card Conspiracy* (Putnam, 1980), Terry Galanoy. A very interesting insider's exposé of some dirty little secrets.

*Credit Card Billing Practices in Virginia* [A report to the General Assembly of Virginia], Charlotte H. Scott, Charlottesville, Tayloe Murphy Institute of the University of Virginia, 1985. Looks at the fairness and unfairness of credit card billing practices. Good information on credit card company billing methods and trickery.

*Credit Card Marketing*, Bill Grady (Wiley, 1995), National Retail Federation Series. A fascinating how-to guide for credit card marketers. Definitely not written from the consumer perspective.

*Credit Card Secrets*, Howard Strong (1989). This is my previous book on the credit card industry. You may find a copy at your local library.

*Expressing America: A Critique of the Global Credit Card Society*, George Ritzer (Thousand Oaks, CA: Pine Forge Press, 1995). Professor Ritzer of the University of Maryland has written a very interesting analysis of the credit card business from a sociological point of view. He suggests that the credit card and fast food industries share many of the same organizing principles. Extensive references to books and articles on the credit card business. This is not a how-to book.

*Give Yourself Credit: A Guide to Consumer Credit Laws*, Subcommittee on Consumer Affairs and Coinage of the Committee on Banking, Finance and Urban Affairs, U.S. House of Representatives (Washington, D.C., January, 1992), Committee Print 102-4, 102nd Congress, 2nd Session. Slightly out-of-date, but still a valuable and *free* resource with the text of many of the federal credit card laws and extensive explanations of those laws; the price is right, no charge, on request from your congressional representative or your senator.

*The Privacy Rights Handbook: How to Take Control of Your Personal Information*, Beth Givens and the Privacy Rights Clearinghouse (Avon Books, 1997). An excellent paperback guide with lots of credit information. Updates to book on the Net at www.privacyrights.org.

*Theft of Identity: The Consumer X-Files II*, California Public Interest Research Group, Los Angeles (1997), is available for $20. CalPIRG's address is in the Organizations section. Also on U.S. PIRG's Website at www.pirg.org.

*Truth in Lending*, 3rd ed., 1995, and annual supplements, Kathleen E. Keest and Gary Klein, National Consumer Law Center, 18 Tremont St., Boston, MA 02108. This is the best technical book on credit card law from a lawyer's perspective. It contains extensive commentary and analysis, as well as the text of most federal credit card laws and regulations. It is not easy going. Part of the eleven-book Consumer Credit and Sales Legal Practice Series. Price, approximately $100. You may find it in a good law library.

*Who Owns Information*, Anne Wells Branscomb (Basic Books, 1994). Who owns the information the card companies collect about you?

## Periodicals

You can often get a free sample copy on request from the publisher, or you may be able to find some of these in your local central public library or the local law library.

*Consumer Action News*, Consumer Action (San Francisco, address in Organizations listing). Publishes yearly comparisons of credit cards and other consumer information, discusses various consumer credit issues. Emphasizes California issues, but valuable nationwide information as well. Sample copy for stamped, self-addressed long envelope (three first-class stamps).

*Consumer Credit and Truth-in-Lending Compliance Report*, Warren, Gorham & Lamont, 210 South St., Boston, MA. Probably the easiest to understand of the trade newsletters. Tells company execs about new developments in credit law, not just credit cards. Very pro-bank attitude. Very expensive.

*Credit Card Management*, Faulkner & Gray, 11 Penn Plaza, 17th Floor, New York, NY 10001-2006, 800-535-8403. Probably the best general publication on the credit industry, this glossy magazine costs $98 a year. Sometimes special introductory subscription offers are available. You may find *Credit Card Management* in the business reference section of a major library. The Los Angeles Public Library, for example, has it in the central reference department.

*NCLC Reports,* National Consumer Law Center, 18 Tremont Street, Boston, MA, 617-523-8010. Consumer Credit and Usury Edition comes out six times a year, a valuable update on consumer credit law from a pro-consumer perspective. Cost is around $50 a year; may be found in some law libraries.

Covers new developments in credit and consumer law. A good source. Mostly for lawyers.

*Nilsen Report*, 300 Esplanade Dr., Suite 1790, Oxnard, CA 93030, 805-983-0448.

This biweekly newsletter is the most important in the credit card area. Opinionated, costly (over $800/year), and more interested in bank cards than in the other varieties of credit cards. Almost impossible to find in libraries. They will send a few sample copies with a request for subscription information.

*Privacy Journal*, P.O. Box 28577, Providence, RI 02908, 401-274-7861, monthly, $118 a year, sometimes offers special price for students and concerned consumers, $35 a year.

An invaluable probe of attempts to take away your right to privacy with plenty of information about what you can do to protect yourself.

## Organizations

CONSUMER GROUPS

Joining and working with these organizations is an effective way for an individual to lend his or her weight to reform. PIRG has local groups around the country.

U.S. PIRG (the national organization of Public Interest Research Groups), 218 D Street S.E., Washington DC 20003 202-546-9707. Website with list of local PIRG groups around the country you could join at www.pirg.org. E-mail address is uspirg@pirg.org.

California PIRG, 11965 Venice Blvd., Suite 408, Los Angeles, CA 90066-3964, 310-397-3404, Sacramento office 916-448-4516. There are also affiliated public interest research groups in several other states such as Massachusetts; get a list from U.S. PIRG above.

Consumer Action, 116 New Montgomery St., Suite 233, San Francisco, CA 94105, 415-777-9635 (calls taken between 10 A.M. and 2 P.M. PST. Publishes surveys of credit card rates and other consumer information in its informative *Consumer Action News*. Membership is $25 a year. Consumer Action is a worthwhile group to join for any consumer, and, due to the California emphasis of its work, is especially valuable to Californians.

Privacy Rights Clearing House, 1717 Ketter Ave., Suite 105, San Diego, CA 92101, 619-298-3396. Collects and distributes information on consumer privacy rights and problems, and publishes around twenty detailed fact sheets on topics such as "Coping with Identity Theft," "My Social Security Number: How Private Is It," "Paying by Credit Card or Check—What Merchants Can Ask." A complete list of fact sheets is available from the Clearing House. Has a Website which includes information sheets in both English and Spanish at www.privacyrights.org.

CREDIT CARD FRANCHISING ORGANIZATIONS
These are the organizations that run the MasterCard and Visa operations and license the use of their trademarks to the various banks who actually issue the cards.

MasterCard International, 888 Seventh Avenue, New York, NY 10106
Visa USA Inc., P.O. Box 8999, San Francisco, CA 94128-8999

---

**DROP ME A NOTE**

*Please,* if you come across a problem I don't cover, an explanation that is not clear, even (it could happen) a mistake, write me at: Howard Strong, P.O. Box 7100, Beverly Hills, CA 90212-7100 and let me know. With your aid the next book will be clearer and more complete. Thank you for your help.

# Index

Page numbers for box text appear in italic type.